The Invisible World

Greg Laurie

FmG
BOOKS

FmG

BOOKS

CONTENTS

CHAPTER

ANGELS:
God's Secret Agents

An invisible world! It's all around us at this very moment; the unseen world of spiritual reality. It's a world that is inhabited both by God and Satan, by angels and demons. It is the world of heaven and hell and, in many ways, it has more substance than the so-called "real world" in which we live.

The invisible world lasts forever;
this physical world will pass away.

When we die and leave these temporary shells called bodies, we will go to one of two places in this spiritual realm and, until that day, the invisible world will have a dramatic effect on the physical one.

WHAT ABOUT UNSEEN CREATURES?

We really need to investigate this matter more closely since it affects us all. For example:

What about angels?
Do you believe in ghosts?
Do you even think there is a supernatural world?

A poll recently taken by USA Today revealed that among America's teenagers:

- 95 percent believe in at least one supernatural phenomenon;
- of that 95 percent, 74 percent of them believe in angels;
- 50 percent believe in ESP;
- 29 percent believe in witchcraft;
- 22 percent believe in ghosts, and
- 16 percent believe in the Loch Ness Monster!

Those same percentages might well represent the views of many adults, too. Most people hold some belief in . . .

the "unseen" . . .
the supernatural . . .
the Invisible World.

Of course, many of us have watched movies like *Ghostbusters.* We're expected to laugh hilariously at the sight of demon powers doing clever, funny little tricks, but behind all the fantasy, there is a very real work going on — a powerful and invisible work.

WHAT ABOUT ANGELS?

Besides the well-worn images of endearing ghosts and terrifying demons, we are also often faced with another form of fictionalized supernatural beings. Angels have been depicted in both religious and non-religious art forms for centuries. Mysterious and majestic, they are a fascinating subject for study.

3

- What are angels really like?
- Who are these mysterious creatures?
- What do they look like?
- What exactly is their purpose?
- Are they anything like the lovable, bumbling angel in the holiday favorite "It's a Wonderful Life?"
- Do they bear any resemblance to the angel in the movie "Heaven Can Wait?"
- Do they really wear long flowing robes and fly across the sky on long, feathery wings?
- Are they always female, as so often portrayed?
- Do they really play harps? What does the Bible actually say about them?

There are any number of misconceptions about angels. I feel that we tend to dismiss them because of all the familiar caricatures and cliches.

According to the Bible, angels are immensely powerful spirit beings, created by God for a definite function. They not only operate in the world-at-large, doing the work of God, but they also have a very specific series of duties in the lives of followers of Jesus Christ. Let's take a look at angelic activity and find out how often we overlook their work in our lives.

Do you realize that you may well have met an angel? No doubt, you're familiar with the passage of Scripture that says, "Don't forget to entertain strangers for some have entertained angels unaware."

That means an angel could cross your path, and you might not even recognize him as such.

If you did indeed recognize him, no doubt you would treat him with great respect, but suppose a person came into your life who wasn't especially desirable. For instance, you may have encountered a street person who didn't smell very good, or perhaps you were introduced to someone with an odd personality. To treat such a person with regard would be a test of your faith. What a disappointment it would be to find out that you'd been visited by an angel and you didn't have time for him! We can't be sure whether or not we've ever met an angel but one thing is certain, encounters with supernatural beings may be more common than we realize.

As we look into the supernatural realm, we find that angelic activity is constant. Billy Graham, in his book on angels, observes that,

> With lightning speed and noiseless movement, angels pass from place to place. They inhabit the space above us. Some are known to be concerned with our welfare, others are set on our harm. The inspired writers draw aside the curtain and give us a glimpse of this invisible world in order that we may be both encouraged and warned.

We're going to take a peek behind that curtain of the invisible. We're not only going to look at good angels and how they function, we're also going to explore the fearful realm of the fallen angels.

WHAT ABOUT DEMONS?

Have you ever wondered where demons came from? Why would God create something as horrible as a demon? Well, the fact is, He didn't. God didn't create demons as we know them today. Demons are rebellious, fallen angels.

There are only three angels identified by name in the Bible. One is Michael, the Archangel. The angel Gabriel is also mentioned a number of times in scripture. And, of course, there is Lucifer who was a very high-ranking angel before he rebelled against God.

We're going to consider some things about each of the two great heavenly angels. Then later on, we will take a look at Lucifer and the demon powers under his control. We'll find that he is not God's equal, although that's what he would like us to believe. We'll see that he has the advantage of a highly organized, power structure of demon powers who do his bidding. We'll also see what his "Achilles heel" is, what his weaknesses are. Lucifer works along predictable lines. He has definite limitations. Best of all, he has limited time left in the world, and he can be overcome!

5

GOD'S SECRET AGENTS

As far as heavenly angels are concerned, one of the reasons we are not aware of their activity in our lives is because they are very effective. They really are God's secret agents.

I heard of one man who wrote about his conversations with angels. Supposedly, they were giving him a great variety of personal revelations. That sort of thing concerns me. In the Bible, we are never taught to seek out angels. Certainly we shouldn't pray to them or try to make contact with them. Instead, we should pray to God and reserve our worship for Him and Him alone. To put it simply, angels are sent to earth to do God's bidding. They are doing it discreetly and quietly, not seeking to draw attention to themselves. God wants us to give honor and glory to Him, not to angelic beings.

Angels Usually Serve Unseen

Angels are invisible, and they remain that way most of the time except on the very special occasions when God sends them on a special mission or "clothes" them with a human form.

When they appear in all their splendor, they are very beautiful. The description of angels in scripture is certainly awe-inspiring. If we could remove the veil that separates our vision from the unseen spiritual world, at this very moment we would see that there are angels all around us. What an incredible sight that would be! We might be tempted to worship them. On the other hand if we could see the demons, the fallen angels, all around us, we would undoubtedly want to run for cover!

Angels Are Magnificent

The Bible tells us that angels are magnificent. The Apostle John tell us in Revelation 22 that when an angel spoke to him, he was so taken by the angel's beauty that he "fell down and worshipped before the feet of the angel which showed [him] these things and he said to [John], 'Don't do it, for I am your fellow servant. Worship God.'"

This helps us understand Paul's statement,

"If I or an angel from heaven come bringing any other gospel than that which you have already heard let him be accursed."

If a beautiful, awe-inspiring angel were to appear to one of us right now (such as Lucifer in all of his glory), we would be inclined to believe just about anything he said... even if it were a different gospel.

Angels Are Ministers

Among other things, angels are sent into our lives as believers to watch out for us and to protect us. Hebrews 1:14 says, "Are they not all ministering spirits sent forth to minister to those who are the heirs of salvation?"

The next time you're afraid, overcome by your circumstances, read Psalm 91. It will bring comfort to your heart as you understand some of the promises for protection God has made to His children. The Psalm begins,

He that dwells in the secret place of the Most High shall abide under the shadow of the Almighty. I will say of the Lord, He is my refuge, my fortress, my God. In Him will I trust.

Those really are wonderful, comforting words, but they are conditional. Only those who "dwell in the secret place of the Most High shall abide under the shadow of the Almighty." In other words,

- God wants to be your hiding place;
- God wants to be the One you turn to when you're afraid;
- God wants to be the One you go to when you can no longer cope.

The Psalmist said, "When my heart is overwhelmed, lead me to the rock that is higher than I."

God waits for you to run to Him for safety just as a small child would run to his parents in times of danger.

7

IF you are making God your "Refuge";
IF you are making God your "Hiding Place";
IF you are trusting in Him; and
IF you are staying as close to Him as you possibly can,

THEN, He guarantees to "give His angels charge over you to keep you in all your ways. They will hold you up lest you dash your foot against a stone."

What a comforting promise of angelic protection.

Satan misconstrued this particular promise during the time of Jesus' temptation in the wilderness. He said to Jesus,

"Cast yourself off from there because He will send
His angels to watch over you." Jesus replied, "It is
written, thou shalt not tempt the Lord thy God."

What Satan was suggesting that Jesus do was reckless, dangerous, designed to test the Father. Jesus brought the suggestion back into context, "You shall not tempt the Lord your God."

- We can't do reckless, crazy things and expect to receive angelic protection.
- We can't act foolishly and anticipate God's blessing.

There is a vast difference between ...

trusting the Lord and
testing the Lord.

But, as Psalm 91 says, if we are seeking to walk in the center of His will and desire to please Him, then indeed, we are promised angelic protection.

Angels are Warriors

Psalm 34:7 has more to say about angels: "The angel of the Lord encamps round about those that fear Him."

This is illustrated a number of times in the lives of God's people. One of the most dramatic illustrations is found in the Old Testament story of the prophet Elisha.

Early one morning as Elisha and his servant were both still asleep, the entire Syrian army closed in on them. They were surrounded! The servant woke first and he was alarmed. He woke Elisha and said, "Master, what shall we do?"

The Prophet said, "Don't be afraid, for those that are with us are more than those that are with them." Then Elisha prayed, "Lord, open his eyes that he may see."

In that moment, the servant had the privilege of peeking behind the supernatural veil to catch a rare glimpse of the invisible world. The Lord opened his eyes and "he saw the mountain was full of horses and chariots of fire all round about Elisha."

That humbled man saw a host of angelic beings all around him and he realized the truth of his master's words, "Those that are with us are more than those that are with them."

Angels Are a Multitude

That is mathematically true. When Satan led his rebellion from heaven, one–third of the angels went with him. That still leaves two–thirds on our side!

How many angels are there? It's hard to say. One passage in Revelation says "ten thousand times ten thousand" which would mean millions and millions. I don't know how many demons there are either, but I know we have many more angels on the side of believers.

When God decided He must destroy Sodom and Gomorrah just two angels were dispatched, charged with the responsibility of getting Lot and his family out of town. When these powerful beings arrived (note that when they appear in Scripture, angels always appear in a masculine form), these men approached the door of Lot's home and soon the whole city showed up. Men began banging on the door saying, "Lot, send out those two men that we may know them."

In the Hebrew, we are given an insight into what these men of Sodom really wanted. The word there for "know" actually means "to have sexual relations with them." Sodom and Gomorrah were known for sexual perversion, homosexuality being one of the prevalent sins there. The men of the city wanted to have sexual relations with these strangers.

Although they were not threatened by this, the angels did not appreciate it, to say the least. The Bible tells us that they came out and smote the people with blindness so they couldn't see where they were going. What amazes me is Lot's reaction. Eroded morally because of his compromised life in Sodom and Gomorrah, he said to the perverse men of Sodom, "Look, I have these virgin daughters that have never known a man. Take them and do what you will, but leave these men alone." Aren't you glad you weren't one of Lot's daughters?

Lot was embarrassed, and for good reason. Angels see a lot of things of which we are totally unaware! They are able to look behind the scenes. In that case, they saw great evil at work. Then, they delivered Lot. Many times they deliver us too.

Angels Deliver God's Judgment

How powerful are angels? We have in the scripture the story of one particular angel who killed 185,000 of Israel's enemies. Needless to say, you don't want to upset an angel.

On another occasion in the New Testament, Herod the king stood up and gave a great speech. The people began to cry, "It's the voice of a god and not of a man!" Herod began to bask in his people's praise and worship, but the Scripture tells us that an angel of the Lord killed him because he failed to give God the glory. You see, angels are also used to bring judgment.

Not only in history, but also in the Last Days scenario as described in Scripture, angels will be used as God's messengers of judgment. In the final hours of time on earth, they will separate the sheep from the goats.

Not only that, but the high-ranking angel, Michael, will play a key role in the rapture of the church. The Scripture says in I Thessalonians 4:16-17,

> The Lord Himself will descend from heaven with a shout and with the voice of the archangel and the trump of God and the dead in Christ will rise first, then those of us who are alive and remain will be caught up together with them in the clouds, and so we shall ever be with the Lord.

Angels will accompany Jesus Christ when He returns. They will be used in the tribulation period, flying through the heavens proclaiming the everlasting gospel.

Sometimes, I think the Lord would accomplish far more by employing angels for His most important tasks. Yet for some strange reason, God has not chosen angels as His primary messengers. He has chosen ordinary people like those of us who have put our faith in Jesus.

Angels Are God's Servants

It's important to note that angels, as wonderful as they are, do not have the privilege of a personal friendship with God as is available to us. Angels don't know what it is to have Jesus Christ living in them, having cleansed them from their sin. The Bible tells us that the angels watch and wonder as they see what God is doing in the lives of believers. There are certain things we understand about God that even an angel does not know.

God could reach out to humanity by opening up the heavens, poking His face through the clouds and saying, "Hello, down there! I'm God and you're not. Why don't you turn to me right now?" Amazingly, instead of that, He's looking for a person on whose behalf He can show Himself strong.

There are other instances in Scripture of God's work in the lives of believers through the agency of angelic beings. Do you remember the story of Daniel? He would not bow in worship before an earthly king. Instead, he chose only to bow before his God. For this defiance, he was thrown into a lion's den in the middle of some very hungry lions. As Daniel was thrown into the pit, a stone was rolled across the top and no one ever expected to see him again, at least not alive. But, the next morning, when the stone was rolled away, Daniel was alive and well. He said to the king, "My God has sent His angels and has shut the lions' mouths and they have not hurt me."

In the book of Genesis, Jacob was fleeing from the anger of his brother Esau. One night, he was feeling very alone and helpless and he found himself in what we might call "an angelic hot spot." As he drifted off to sleep, Jacob dreamed that he saw a ladder leading to heaven from earth with angels ascending and descending on it! In this way, God confirmed to Jacob He that was with him.

Early in the New Testament, we read how Mary, Jesus' mother, supernaturally conceived the Son of God. That's a tough thing to try and explain to your husband-to-be! Mary had been faithful to Joseph. She had been faithful to God, but she needed a little help to support her unbelievable story. So, an angel appeared to Joseph ... not just any angel! God sent one of the highest ranking angels, Gabriel. Gabriel announced, "Do not be afraid to take Mary as your wife for that which is conceived in her is of the Holy Spirit."

Once again, an angel was sent to the rescue.

Then, there is the story in the book of Acts about the time the Apostle Paul was sailing to Rome as a prisoner. A great storm came up, and everyone aboard the ship was in terror. They despaired for their lives. But the Lord sent an angel to Paul, comforting him with the message that he would not be harmed. Paul was able to say to the people, "An angel has appeared to me and given me this encouragement."

As we ponder these encounters between believers and angels, we recognize that we have no way of knowing how many times angels have:

 delivered us from danger;

gotten us out of tight situations;

protected us from harm; or

spoken directly to us.

Some of the times you've sensed the Lord speaking to you, He may have spoken through an angel. An angel may have rescued you from a difficult circumstance. Many times, we narrowly escape disaster. No doubt, an angel protected us. They're active. They're busy.

12

Angels Are Sent When We Pray

Another exciting story of angelic intervention in Acts 12:1-5 tells us how angelic activity and prayer can work together.

> Now about that time, King Herod stretched out his hand to harass some from the church. And he killed James the brother of John with the sword. Because he saw that it pleased the Jews, he also proceeded to seize Peter. It was during the days of unleavened bread. When he had arrested him, he put him in prison and delivered him to four squads of soldiers to keep him, intending to bring him before the people after Passover. Peter was therefore kept in prison but constant prayer was offered to God for him by the church.

James had been killed, and Herod was aware that his murder had pleased the religious Jews. So he seized Simon Peter and imprisoned him. He kept him under the watchful eye of four squads of guards. Herod didn't want another impossible-to-explain episode like the the resurrection of Jesus! What an embarrassment it had been when Jesus rose from the dead! It was still a popular topic of conversation even though the Romans had slanderously spread the rumor that His disciples had stolen Jesus' body.

Worse yet, as far as Herod was concerned, Peter had already been rescued from prison once before by an angel. Now this time, Herod was taking no chances. He was going to make sure Peter didn't get out of the slammer. Peter was locked up behind two gates, chained to two guards and protected by fourteen more. There was no way he would escape this time, or so Herod thought; however, he had not taken into consideration the supernatural element, The Invisible World.

What did the Church do? Under such difficult circumstances, knowing Peter was imprisoned, did they go down and picket the prison or launch a letter-writing campaign? No. Actually, they used their secret weapon, prayer, the weapon that can penetrate any wall. Though the prison doors remained closed, another door remained open. It was the door of prayer, the door into the very presence of God.

Often we hear it said after every other possibility has been exhausted, "Well, all I can do now is (gulp!) pray." That really bothers me. Praying is what we should do in the first place! Let us not insult God.

Also, it is evidence of our ignorance in regard to the power of God and His willingness to assist us. James said, "You have not because you ask not."

How many times do we hit brick walls in our lives, when obstacles are not removed because we simply fail to believe God's promise to answer prayer? He's waiting for us to cry out to Him.

God allows certain events in our lives to cause us to trust Him and to prevent us from trusting in ourselves or other people. When we fail to seek His help, we miss the blessings He has in store.

Jesus said, "Ask and it shall be given you. Seek and you shall find. Knock and the door shall be opened."

During Peter's imprisonment, the believers in Acts took this literally. They began to ask, seek and knock through the avenue of prayer. Notice that it says in Acts 12:5, "Constant prayer was offered to God for him by the church."

This word "constant" could be translated "earnest and intense prayer" or they were "stretched out in prayer." Have you ever extended yourself just as far as possible to reach something beyond your grasp? Those faithful Christians were stretching out in prayer to God.

Satan wanted Peter dead.

God wanted Peter alive.

The spiritual battle lines were drawn; the Church prayed with all its might. You can fight and win battles in prayer without ever lifting a finger. Never underestimate God's power.

In another story, the bitter conflict between the angelic forces of God and the fallen angels that oppose Him is vividly described. This glimpse into the spiritual realm, the Invisible World, shows us what happens behind the scenes when we pray. The story unfolds as the prophet, Daniel, is praying for a certain thing. We read that his prayer was immediately heard and that God dispatched an angel with the answer. This was an angel with a specific message in answer to Daniel's prayer.

However, the angel was unable to reach Daniel. He was engaged by a demon power that stopped him. As a matter of fact, the angel was hindered for twenty-one days by this evil creature. The demon power was apparently of a higher position than the angel was. Certainly, it is clear in other scriptures that there are rankings in angelic forces. Scripture tells us that we are not fighting "against flesh and blood but against principalities and powers" and "rulers of darkness."

In any case, this demon power was able to stop an angel. So, God sent Michael, the Archangel. It's quite foolish to stand against an angel, much less an angel of Michael's caliber. Michael arrived on the scene, set the lower–ranking angel free and brought Daniel the answer to his prayer.

I find this an interesting story. Prayer was offered to God and it took twenty-one days for the answer to come. We can see that when we pray and our prayers aren't immediately answered, we shouldn't conclude that God isn't listening. This Bible revelation makes it clear that "Delays are not necessarily denials." There is a battle raging. Keep that in mind when you pray.

If you're interceding with God for the salvation of a loved one, you're doing spiritual battle on your knees. Satan doesn't want your loved one to come to Christ.

Perhaps you invited a friend to church only to get back a flimsy excuse. Did you persist and extend the invitation again? This time, car trouble came from nowhere! Another invitation ... only to hear of illness. Do you wonder if this precious person will ever make it to church? Pray about it. Don't try to make it happen on your own. Ask God to open the doors so that your friend will hear the gospel. Realize that you're engaged in spiritual warfare and the devil's going to do everything he can to stop you. But you're on the right side! You're praying according to the will of God: "He is not willing that any should perish but that all should come to repentance (II Peter 3:9)."

15

Now, back to our story. What happened when the early church prayed? We read in Acts 12,

> Now behold an angel of the Lord stood by Peter and a light shone in the prison and he struck Peter on the side. "Wake up," he said and the chains fell off his hands. Then the angel said, "Gird yourself up, tie on your sandals and put on your garment and follow me."

Peter groggily went out, following this angelic deliverer, but he wasn't sure if all this was really happening. He thought he was seeing a vision. When they were past the first and second guard post, they came to the iron gate of the prison which opened for them of its own accord. They stepped out onto the street and immediately the angel departed from Peter.

In all his rejoicing, Peter remembered that the Church was praying. Verse 12 says,

> When he had considered this, he came to the house of Mary the mother of John, whose surname was Mark; where many were gathered together praying.

Most likely, they were specifically praying for Peter's deliverance. So Peter knocked at the door of the gate and a girl named Rhoda answered. She recognized Peter's voice. She was so excited, she didn't even open the gate! Instead, she ran into the prayer meeting and announced that Peter was standing outside the gate. What did those men of great faith, who were praying fervently for Peter's deliverance, say? "You're crazy, Rhoda!"

Possibly, these men of God had just prayed, "Father, deliver Peter. We know You can do it. We know You have sufficient power. One of Your angels killed 185,000 Syrians. We remember the story of how You sent an angel to shut the lions' mouths for your servant Daniel. Now we ask You to get our beloved friend and leader, Peter, out of prison."

Their prayer was interupted and they were informed that Peter was standing at the front door. They couldn't believe it! To remind us that men and women of the Bible were not perfect, we have this illustration, and others.

Rhoda stubbornly insisted that it was so. They concluded that it was his angel. If Peter's angel had been knocking at the door, shouldn't they let him in?

Peter continued knocking. The doors opened wide for him in the prison but he couldn't get through the door to his friends' house! Peter may have been worried about being recaptured by the authorities if he didn't get off the street. Of course, eventually the believers welcomed him inside and they all rejoiced as he told them what God had done.

Why did God deliver Peter and not James?

James was killed; Peter was spared.

We might ask a similar question: why do angels protect some and allow others to die? Tragedy is not foreign to Christians. We have all seen lives that seem to have been cut short. We don't understand why. We think,

- "Lord, weren't You paying attention?"
- "Why wasn't an angel dispatched to stop that from happening? "
- "Why didn't You do something?"

We must realize that angels are not only meant to protect, deliver and minister to us. They have another role as well.

They are responsible to accompany us to heaven some day. For every believer there comes the moment when our number is up. Life is over. It's possible that we may live to a ripe old age, or we may not live much longer at all. We don't know when the time will come, but God certainly does. Our days are numbered.

Until that day, angels are responsible to protect us, watch over us and minister to us. Then, when the day comes for us to pass from time into eternity, angels will make sure we get there safely and quickly. God commissions angels to escort each believer to heaven and to give each one a royal welcome as he enters the eternal presence of God. Every one of us who has trusted Jesus Christ as our Lord and Savior will have this angelic escort.

In the book of Acts, we read of a man named Stephen who was boldly standing up for what he believed, sharing the message of the gospel with Jewish religious leaders. As he was speaking to them, they saw his face "as if it had become the face of an angel." I don't know exactly what that means, but in our mind's eye, we can see a radiant face shining as it reflects the glory of God.

17

It almost appears that while Stephen spoke, he was beginning to see into the supernatural realm, the Invisible World. As he continued to preach, the people listening became enraged with the truthfulness of his message. They put their fingers in their ears and screamed because they didn't want to hear what he was saying. Soon they were running toward him, throwing stones at him. Before long, he lay dying.

As Stephen's young life drained away and his spirit left his body, he said, "Look, I see the heavens open and the Son of man standing on the right hand of God." The angels were already "airlifting" him out of there. As he was leaving, he exclaimed, "Look, I see Jesus standing...."

Interesting, isn't it, that usually when we read of Jesus in heaven, He's sitting on the right hand of God? Yet in this instance, He's standing. I believe He was extending a hero's welcome to this young man who had so bravely given his all. The angels lifted Stephen up and carried him directly into the presence of God.

Death for the Christian cuts the cord that holds us captive in this present evil world. We needn't be afraid of death. D. L. Moody, the great evangelist, had this deathbed experience as recorded in a book written by his son.

> There on his deathbed, he was aware death was at hand and he said, "Earth is receding and the heavens are opening before me." It was like he was dreaming. Then he said, "No, this is no dream. It's beautiful. It's like a trance. If this is death, it is sweet. There is no valley here. God is calling me. I must go." He closed his eyes and they thought he was dead. Then he opened his eyes and said he'd seen beyond the thin veil separating the seen from the unseen world. He had been within the gates and beyond the portals and had caught a glimpse of familiar faces whom he had loved long since and lost awhile. Then Moody died and went into the presence of God.

In his book, *Angels*, Billy Graham writes about his maternal grandmother. He reports that he was in the room with her at the time of her death. The room seemed to fill with a heavenly light, she sat up in her bed, almost laughing, and said, "I see Jesus. He has His arms outstretched towards me. I see Ben (her husband who had died some years earlier). And I see angels." Then, she slumped over, absent from the body but present with the Lord.

Billy also mentions in that same book, that while he was a student in Bible school, a missionary volunteer was suddenly stricken with illness on the campus. The physician said that the young woman only had a few hours to live. Her husband, along with one or two faculty members were in the room when she suddenly exclaimed, "I see Jesus! I hear the singing of angels!"

You see, when we pass into the presence of God, it's glorious! It's our reward. It's what we've been waiting for. It's not something to fear or dread. Jesus died on the cross and rose again from the dead so we wouldn't have to fear death. He's been to the other side and He's saying, "Come on in, the water's fine. I've checked it out for you. There's nothing to worry about. I'm waiting for you."

Jesus' death cleared a road through Satan's kingdom; a safe way for us to come into His eternal presence and He provided angelic protection for us from the very real demon forces who want to keep us from entering into glory.

You might respond, "Come on. Give me a break. Do you really believe all this about a supernatural world?" You bet I do! The spiritual world is very real. Demon forces want to pull you away from Christ and keep you from coming to Him. If you're a believer, they want to drag you into sin. Even when we're on our deathbeds, they'd love to snatch us away but Jesus said, "You are my sheep and no man will pluck you out of my hand."

You're in good hands with Jesus Christ. Satan can't lay one finger on you.

Don't tell me to fear death.

Don't tell me to attempt to prolong my life.

Don't tell me to run from eternity.

For a believer, "To live is Christ and to die is gain."

■ Death is graduation.

■ Death is a coronation.

It's a reward by which we pass from this decaying body into the eternal body that God has prepared for us. That's the hope for every Christian.

There is life after death for everyone, non-Christian as well as Christian. That life either will be eternal separation from God in hell or eternal blessing and reward in the presence of God in heaven.

Clearly, the Lord wants us to be with Him in heaven. He wants to share eternity with us. He is so excited about it, He's willing to send an angelic escort to usher us into His presence.

I can hardly wait, can you?

THE INVISIBLE WORLD

C H A P T E R

Facts About Fallen Angels

Having seen an overview of the role of good angels in the life of the believer, let's examine the fallen or bad ones. In Ephesians 6:10-13, Paul writes,

> "Finally, my brothers, be strong in the Lord, and in the power of His might. Put on the whole armor of God, that you may be able to stand against the deceits and strategies of the devil. For we are not wrestling against flesh and blood, but against principalities, against powers, against the rulers of the darkness of this world, against spiritual wickedness in the heavenly places."

I hope you're beginning to gain a better understanding of what is taking place in the supernatural realm; what I call the Invisible World. Though we cannot see it with our physical eyes, that doesn't make it any less real. Right now, even as we are considering this subject, there is a spiritual battle raging all around us. There are angels of God and demons under Satan's direction; both are powerful and active.

SATAN PLANS OUR DESTRUCTION

In the last chapter, we examined the purpose and work of God's holy angels in the believer's life. On the other side of the unseen world is a dark and evil realm inhabited by fallen angels. If you want to know the intentions of fallen angels, demons and Satan, one of the best definitions is given by Jesus, himself, in John 10:10. He said,

> "I have come that you might have life and that more abundantly. In contrast, the thief [Satan] comes only to kill, steal and destroy."

That's what the devil wants to do. He wants to kill you. He wants to steal you away from the protection and blessing of God. He wants to destroy you. Demons do his bidding and help him accomplish his purposes. When we say, "The devil really tempted me the other day," it's quite unlikely that it was actually the devil, although he would love for us to think about him in those terms.

How Strong Is He?

◼ God is omnipotent: all–powerful.

◼ He's omniscient: all–knowing.

◼ He's omni-present: everywhere at the same time.

◼ The devil is not all–knowing; his knowledge is incomplete.

◼ He is not all–powerful; his power is limited.

◼ He's not present everywhere; he's in only one place.

23

If he's in San Francisco, he can't be in Los Angeles. If he's in Los Angeles, he can't be in New York City or wherever he's going to make his next call. Actually, he is nowhere near God's equal.

He does send forth his satanic regiments, the demon forces, to accomplish his work and the effect is, by and large, the same. Satan has an extremely well–organized group of demon powers working for him. Look again at Ephesians 6:12, which says:

> We're not wrestling against flesh and blood, but against principalities, powers, rulers of the darkness of this age, spiritual hosts of wickedness, in the heavenly realm.

Do you see all the distinctions?

There are principalities.
There are powers.
There are rulers.
There are spiritual hosts.

I don't claim to understand how this all operates, because the Bible is largely silent about it. We don't really need to know the inner workings of all the demon powers. The Bible tells us enough about them to enable us to deal with them.

The Angels Respect His Power

There are also distinctions made in angelic ranks, including higher and lower–ranking angels. Michael is probably the highest–ranking of the angels. Gabriel may or may not be Michael's equal, but he is also a high-ranking angel who is mentioned by name. Lucifer, the prince of the power of the air, is the highest–ranking fallen angel; he is Satan himself.

An interesting meeting between Lucifer and Michael is recorded in Jude 1:9. It says,

> Michael the archangel, in contending with the devil when he disputed about the body of Moses, did not bring against him a reviling accusation, but said, "The Lord rebuke you."

I wonder what that was all about! The Bible doesn't tell us anymore, but somewhere in history Michael and Lucifer went toe–to–toe. I don't know why they were fighting over the body of Moses nor what the devil wanted to do with it. But Michael was standing against Lucifer, and the important point is that Michael did not "bring a railing accusation" against Lucifer. Instead, he simply said, "The Lord rebuke you." Some people foolishly fail to follow Michael's example and do just the opposite!

We Must Respect His Power

I become very uneasy when I hear people calling the devil silly names; challenging him, in a way, by making fun of him. I wouldn't do that. I have a healthy respect for my adversary. If Michael the archangel, with all of his power and spiritual prestige, did not bring any kind of accusation against the devil, why should I? When it comes to spiritual warfare, it is vitally important for us to stand in God's strength and not in our own. By the way, Michael will ultimately triumph over Satan in the future, overcoming his old rival in the last battle.

HE HAD A BEGINNING

You might say, "Wait a minute. You speak about demons and Satan. Where did Satan actually come from? And why would a loving

God ever have created a horrible creature such as Lucifer? Why would He have created demons as well? How did this come about?"

Remember that God did not create the devil as we know him today. God originally created a spirit being, an angel of great wisdom and beauty. He lived in heaven in a position of great power and influence. Perhaps the devil was even an archangel once. Lucifer is described in Ezekiel 28:15, "You're perfect in your ways from the day you were created. Until iniquity was found in you."

Another translation says,

You had the seal of perfection. You were full of wisdom. Perfect in beauty. But your heart was lifted up because of your beauty. You corrupted your wisdom by reason of your brightness. I will cast you to the ground.

Isaiah 14:12-15 says,

How you are fallen from heaven, oh Lucifer son of the morning. How you are cut to the ground for you said in your heart "I will ascend unto heaven. I will exalt my throne above the stars of God. I will ascend above the heights of the clouds. I will be like the most High."

God said, "You will be brought down to hell."
Jesus said, "I beheld Satan fall as lightning to the earth."

Lucifer, this glorious son of the morning, this high-ranking, powerful angel, decided he did not want to worship God. Instead he wanted to be worshiped himself, and consequently he lost his position among the angels of God. As mentioned in Revelation 12, we read about the dragon, identified as Satan, taking one–third of the "stars" with him to earth. We are told in Revelation that those stars refer to the angels. One–third of the angelic ranks followed Lucifer in his rebellion against God. Of that one–third, some demons are imprisoned right now. Jude 6 says,

And the angels who did not keep their proper domain but left their own abode he has reserved in everlasting chains under darkness for the judgment of the great day.

Why one group of demons is imprisoned and one group isn't, remains a mystery, but those that are free to do Satan's bidding are certainly doing an effective job. We have many references to the agenda and activity of demons and fallen angels in the New Testament.

GOD PLACES LIMITS ON SATAN

Concerning demons, there are two extremes that must be shunned. First, we must avoid the tendency to see a demon behind every tree. Some people are so obsessed with demonic activity that it's ridiculous. They think everything that happens to them has been caused by a demon. Every impure thought they have, every problem they confront, every mistake they make, they blame on demonic influence. These people are unwilling to accept responsibility for their own actions. Instead they rationalize, "The devil made me do it."

It's very unhealthy to focus too much attention on demons. I think they enjoy the "PR." They are thoroughly delighted when someone dedicates an entire church service to casting out demons in some sort of exorcism rite. They love the attention, and delight in getting credit for a lot of things they had nothing to do with. We must reject the extreme perspective that sees demons everywhere, in everything.

On the other hand, we must avoid treating the existence of demons with unbelief and mockery. It's foolish to say, "No, they're not even there. It's not real. It's all a joke. It's a figment of your imagination!" I assure you on the authority of scripture that they're out there and they're active.

 The first error in thinking can lead to fanatical fear.

The second can lead to a false security.

Both attitudes are dangerous.

I Timothy 4:1 says,

> The Spirit speaks clearly that in the last days there will be satanically energized times and some will fall, depart from the faith giving heed to seducing spirits and doctrines of demons.

His Activity Will Increase

In the last days, demonic activity will be commonplace and intensified. The devil knows his number is almost up! He knows his judgment is certain. He knows there is an impending doom waiting for him. He believes (even if some liberal theologions don't) that Jesus is, indeed, coming again. Therefore, he's pulling out all the stops. He's redoubling his efforts. He's going for the jugular. His objective is to take as many people to hell with him as possible. He knows he's going there and he would like to drag as many victims with him as he possibly can.

He Always Opposes the Gospel

Satan absolutely loathes any activity on the part of the church to spread the gospel. If you've made a personal commitment to Jesus Christ, it's bad enough that he's lost you. He's still unhappy about that, to say the least. But, the fact that now you want to go out and win other people to Christ really is a matter of grave concern to him. Satan opposes any efforts of Christians to share their faith. That is why whenever we choose to be used of God, we should brace ourselves for spiritual opposition. Whenever I start getting a lot of Satanic opposition it reminds me that I'm on the right track. He's trying to stop me!

Satan's Demons Sometimes Possess People

In the New Testament, we read about individuals who are possessed by demons. Is it possible for a person to be possessed by a demon today? Will his head turn around like the girl in the movie *The Exorcist*? I didn't see *The Exorcist*, but I've talked to people who have told me how frightening it was. It dealt with the very real unseen world and it frightened a lot of people. Of course, in movies like *Ghostbusters*, we think it's kind of cute when the little demons come and "slime" people. "Who ya gonna call? Ghostbusters!" You can stop by the local toy store and find all of the cute little demon toys you could ever want for your children. It's all very charming.

It is also quite frightening and even dangerous. It troubles me when I see some of the merchandise which is available for children in toy stores today. Please understand, I don't see demons under every bush, but when I see figures that are designed to look like demons, it disturbs me. I was in a toy store a while back and a book was prominently displayed that related to the series, "Dungeons and Dragons." On the cover was the picture of a naked woman lying on an altar, apparently illustrating some sort of sacrifice described in the text. "What is this doing in a toy store?" I asked myself. "What is this doing to the innocent, impressionable minds of children?"

28

He Traps the Unwary

Many Saturday morning cartoons are filled with the occult, as well. I know that if we start nit-picking, it becomes difficult to live in the "real world"; however, when we're faced with blatantly demonic products that encourage children to be fascinated by evil, we should be more than concerned. We really should seek to protect our children from them.

As kids get older, they are confronted with heavy metal music. This style of rock 'n roll is filled with words that aren't the least bit subtle; many blatantly promote devil worship. You'll see pentagrams on the stage; the number 666 on record covers and T-shirts. These groups adopt satanic symbols that will produce the greatest shock value, and wear them for that very purpose. What the young fans don't realize, however, is that they are actually dabbling with some very real supernatural dangers although they rationalize listening and displaying these symbols and emblems. The results can be horrifying and tragic.

He Ruins Lives

In researching a book I've written on teen suicide, I found that for many of these hopeless kids, the door to death opened through such activity. If you're not a Christian, you are open game for the devil and his demons. You're a sitting duck. You have no protection, no defense mechanisms, no place to hide. Satan can do with you pretty much as he will. The Bible says in the book of II Timothy that Satan is able to come and take you, against your will, to do his will.

In the Gospels, we find demon-possessed people experiencing such symptoms as blindness, dumbness, and insanity. I'm not suggesting that every blind, dumb, or insane person is demon–possessed. I am saying those symptoms happened as a result of demon activity in the New Testament.

He Sends Demons in Groups

One man lived among the tombs in the country of the Gadarenes. He was possessed by a large number of demons and had superhuman strength. Sometimes he cut himself with rocks and, if someone tried to control him by chaining him, he simply broke the chains. He was a wild man. One day, Jesus came walking along. The Gadarene man saw Him from a distance and the demon-spirit cried out, "What have I to do with you Jesus, Son of the most high God? Do not torment me!" Interesting. Even demons know the power of Jesus Christ. Jesus said, "Come out of the man, you unclean spirit!"

Jesus asked the spirit's name and the spirit replied, "Legion, for we are many." By the way, this is the only time in the Bible that a demon gave its name. Jesus allowed the demons to enter into a herd of pigs. The demons drove the pigs over the side of a cliff and they drowned. Those were demon-possessed pigs; you might even say they were deviled ham!

What can we learn about fallen angels from this story? First of all, we see that when people are possessed by demons they can have superhuman strength. I have seen demon-possessed people. I've prayed for them. I remember *dealing* with people who were possessed and had superhuman strength.

Demons Recognize the Name of Jesus

In the book of Acts, we read about a fascinating little group of guys who were called the sons of Sceva. They were sort of traveling exorcists. The Bible does not approve of this ministry, by the way. It doesn't even say they were believers. Yet, they felt they could go around and cast demons out of people. One day, they came across a demon-possessed man, walked up to him, and said, "We exorcise you by the name of Jesus whom Paul preaches." The evil spirit answered, "Jesus I know, and Paul I know, but I don't know who you are!" At that point, the demon-possessed man leaped on them, overpowered them and prevailed against them. They ran out of the house naked and wounded. I'll bet they never did that again!

The demon speaking through this man said, "I've heard of Jesus, definitely. I've even heard of Paul, but who do you think you are?" These self-proclaimed exorcists didn't do the job in the power of Jesus and it got them into a lot of trouble. This shows us the supernatural power of demons and the futility of engaging in spiritual warfare in our own strength. That's why we read in Ephesians 6:10, "Be strong in the Lord and in the power of His might."

I hear some wild-eyed preachers talk about their spiritual exploits. They tell us they have been personally fighting the devil, doing warfare with him. They can go ahead and fight the devil all they want. I'm not interested. I'm not interested in chasing demons. I'm not interested in engaging in a personal battle with them because they could wipe me out. All I'm interested in is standing in the Lord and in the power of His might. I'll let Him do the fighting for me!

Demons Can Cause Suicide

It's obvious, as we've pointed out, that demon possession is real. Possession occurs when Satan takes control of a person. In the case of the Gadarene demoniac, suicidal tendencies resulted. The Bible says he cut himself. As I mentioned, a large number of today's teenagers are taking their own lives. This phenomenon represents an epidemic that has been unknown in our country until recently. Every year, 600,000 teenagers try to commit suicide. Some experts believe the number is far higher. Ten percent of these teenagers succeed in their attempt to take their own lives.

What drives these kids to such radical measures? I've done some extensive study into this heartbreaking subject, and there are many reasons given. A good portion of these children have been deceived by Satan himself, and are driven by him toward self-destruction. The enemy is active. He's alive, and he's making lots of progress in these difficult times in which we live.

Demons and Drugs

Often the kids with suicidal tendencies have been overtaken by evil powers because they've dabbled with drugs. There is a definite link between drugs and the occult. The Bible warns of the sin of sorcery. The word "sorcery" comes from the Greek word "pharmekia" from which we get our English word pharmacy. The biblical definition of sorcery has to do with the illicit use of drugs. When people begin to use drugs, whether it's marijuana, cocaine, or any other mind-controlling substance, it opens them up to the spiritual realm. Dabbling in black magic, witchcraft, Ouija boards or astrology can also open the door.

CAN A CHRISTIAN BE DEMON POSSESSED?

What about demon-possessed Christians? We hear of churches that hold services supposedly for the purpose of casting demons out of Christian believers. I received an interesting letter from an individual who was attending a church where the pastor claimed to be casting demons out of Christians every week. This pastor had gone so far as to even publish an index of different demons! That way, you could determine which one might be troubling you. The man who wrote to me was frustrated and left the church, but before he left, he got a copy of the index and mailed it to me. Here was an inventory, probably about 30 pages long, of all the demons that theoretically could possess people, even Christians.

It listed the demons you might expect to see. The index stated that there were demons of:

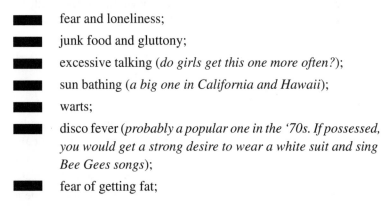

- fear and loneliness;
- junk food and gluttony;
- excessive talking (*do girls get this one more often?*);
- sun bathing (*a big one in California and Hawaii*);
- warts;
- disco fever (*probably a popular one in the '70s. If possessed, you would get a strong desire to wear a white suit and sing Bee Gees songs*);
- fear of getting fat;

- "cool" or trying to be cool;
- going on a spending spree;
- food gulping; and
- baldness!

I must admit to you, I found myself laughing out loud as I read this nonsense. This is absurd! You can talk about demons of lust or impure thoughts or gluttony, but I've got another name for it. It's called "The Flesh." You don't need to cast it out; you need to die to it! It's really easy to say "The devil made me do it." A demon took control, but the Bible says, "To whom you yield yourselves as servants to obey, his servants you are." We make decisions to commit certain acts. We can choose to steal, lie or lose our tempers. There's no point in saying demons make us do these things! It is our responsibility. A demon cannot do anything in the life of a Christian unless the Christian cooperates. As Christians, the devil can tempt us. Demons can harass us. They can even oppress us, but they cannot possess us or take control of us.

Not All Claims are Scriptural

I read another popular book about Christians who supposedly have been possessed; the term the author used was "demonized." This individual claimed that he was able to determine when a person was possessed because he could see a vision of reptiles or spiders on the area of the body where the possession was occurring. If he saw spiders and reptiles around the head, for example, it indicated that the person was having problems with his thoughts. If he saw such a vision, he immediately cast out the demons. It's all very fascinating, and it's all completely unscriptural. Nowhere in the Bible, apart from the one time the demon called itself Legion, do we read of any demon giving its name.

Not All "Experts" Can Be Trusted

What is this business about engaging in extended conversations with demons? What's the point? I read one particular manual where the author wrote on how to cast out demons. He says, "When the demon comes out you're going to throw up because a demon has lodged itself in you." So, when men and women come to his church, little handkerchiefs are given to them, and the next thing you know, people are throwing up. What a meaningful time with God that must be.

What foolishness! I think the enemy is quite pleased with all this activity. Under such circumstances, would I come into church thinking about God and His power? No. My mind would be fixed on Satan and his demons. "What demon got you this week? Oh, gluttony got you? Well, warts got me. You know what? I think you are possessed by the demon of bad breath, and I'm getting the demon of gluttony; let's go eat. Give me a break!

JESUS IS OUR DEFENSE

I think these demons enjoy the attention. Here's the truth of the matter: Jesus Christ dealt the decisive blow against Satan and his demonic forces at the Cross of Calvary. He cried three words from the cross that forever turned the tide of events in the spiritual world. Those words were, "It is finished." Colossians 3 says that at the Cross, Jesus spoiled, deprived of power, all principalities and powers. He made an open show of them by triumphing over them. As a Christian, I don't have to fear that Satan will get hold of my life.

Jesus, speaking of his power of demons, said in Luke 11:21,

"When a strong man, fully armed, guards his palace,
his goods are at peace but when one stronger than he
comes along and overcomes him he takes from him
all his armor in which he trusted and divides his
spoil."

Jesus Is Stronger Than Satan

Satan was the strong man in our lives at one time. He held us under lock and key, but a stronger man came—Jesus Christ. He overcame the enemy, took away his weapons and divided his spoils. Jesus delivered us alive from the clutches of Satan. We're now free from him and his power. "He who the Son sets free is free indeed," Jesus said. The Scripture tells us that once Christ comes into our lives, "Greater is He who is in you than he who is in the world."

33

Jesus Will Outlive Satan

As I have pointed out, Satan knows his time is limited. Evil spirits know their final end is coming. They're trying to do as much harm and wreak as much havoc as they can in these present days. I'm so thankful to have Christ living inside me. I don't have to run around in fear of what the devil's going to do.

I'm not looking for the devil... I'm looking for the Lord.

I'm not looking for the Antichrist... I'm looking for Jesus Christ.

I'm not looking for the Adversary... I'm looking to my Advocate.

Jesus is my Advocate, my Defense Attorney. He's the Author and Finisher of my faith. I'm concentrating on Him and, as a result of that, I don't have to fear what the devil's going to do next.

Jesus Drives Demons Away

We're told in I John 5:18, "If a man is born of God, the wicked one touches him not." That phrase "touches him not" means the wicked cannot attach himself to the believer. Those who say we can be demon–possessed or demonized are speaking from an unscriptural position. Jesus is not into a "time-share program" when it comes to His children. When He enters into a life, He is the sole resident. There is no room for the devil or demons to cohabit there. When the Lord rules, He rules completely, but those who are not Christians are open prey.

If I were not a believer however, I would be very frightened right now. This world is really getting crazy. Look at the bizarre things that are happening; the crimes; the incredible mass murders; the sick perversions. Things that would have shocked us ten years ago have become commonplace today. Yet as Christians, we're protected and safe, as long as we stay close to the Lord and abide in Him (John 15).

When Jesus died on the cross, He did not only die to deal the decisive blow to Satan. He also died to forgive men and women of their sins. The Bible says that Satan has blinded the eyes of those that do not believe lest the light of the gospel should shine on them. Some people are never really able to see spiritually. When they are presented with their need for Jesus Christ, it just doesn't penetrate. They don't get it. I remember the day my eyes were opened spiritually. Prior to that, I'd heard about Christ. People had given me little religious booklets to read and I'd watched television preachers, but the message had never penetrated my hardened heart.

Then one day, it suddenly made sense. I realized that I was a sinner and I needed to know Jesus. I asked Him to forgive my sins and to come into my life. Up to that point, I hadn't realized that such a thing was even possible. Sometimes people say, "I believe in God. I acknowledge His existence." That's not enough! The Bible says, "The demons believe and tremble." We must believe and then act upon it by receiving His salvation. The Bible says, "As many as receive Him, to them He gave the power to become the sons of God."

Jesus stands at the door and knocks. If we'll open the door, He will come in and once He has become Lord and Savior, we are rescued from the forces of darkness. We no longer have reason to tremble at the thought of Satan. We are not prey for his wicked, fallen angels.

35

If you have not done so yet, why don't you bow your head in prayer right now and ask Jesus Christ to forgive you of your sin, and become your Lord and Savior?

He loves you ... and He's only a prayer away.

THE INVISIBLE WORLD

CHAPTER

3

*What The Devil
Doesn't Want You
To Know*

I t is my firm conviction that we are living in the Last Days. By that, I mean that Bible prophecies are being fulfilled and, as a result, Jesus Christ could come back any time!

Also, it's obvious to me that the enemy is stepping up his efforts. He's become far more blatant than ever before and not nearly as subtle as he used to be. Yet at the same time, there is also a powerful moving of God's spirit. Romans 13:11-12 says,

> Knowing the critical, strategic period of time, it's time for us as believers to wake out of our sleep for now is our salvation nearer than when we believed. The night is far spent. The day is at hand. Let us, therefore, cast off once and for all the works of darkness and put on the armor of light.

We need to wake up and realize that we are living in strategic and very critical times. Clearly, these are not days for playing games with God and living with a half-hearted commitment to Him. The only way to survive spiritually in today's world is to be completely sold out to Jesus Christ. Otherwise, we are going to be sitting ducks for the tactics, strategies and flaming arrows of hell.

We need to have a realistic concept of who this spirit being that we call Satan really is. On one hand, we don't want to underestimate the devil. He is a sly and skillful foe. After all, he's been perfecting his craft for 6,000 years of dealings with mankind, and he has the tricks of his trade well-honed. Yet on the other hand, we don't want to overstate his capabilities. We need to look at him rationally and understand exactly who he is and what we are dealing with. I'm going to share with you a few things I think the devil doesn't want you to know.

SUPERNATURAL POWER

First on the list is the fact that he has definite limitations. He would love for us to think he is the equal of God; that as God rules from heaven, the devil rules from hell; that whatever God can accomplish, the devil can, too, and that they are equals, fighting over the souls of men. That simply isn't true. God certainly does rule from heaven, but the devil does not rule from hell. The devil hasn't even been to hell yet, and he is far from being God's equal. We've all seen caricatures or cartoons in which the devil is seated on a big, fiery throne in the midst of hell's flames. All the little demons with their horns and pitchforks report in each day, receive their orders and head out into the world to do his bidding. This is frightening, ominous and completely false.

Satan Is Not Omniscient

Remember, Satan is not God's equal, not by any stretch of the imagination. Satan has been granted power, and it is more than has been given to any man, but that power is restricted. Satan is not omniscient, or all-knowing. In contrast, God knows everything about you. He knows what you're going to think before you think it. He knows where you're going to go before you leave to get there. He knows the future better than you and I know the past. Satan's knowledge is incomplete. He would like us to think he is all knowing but, although he is clever and has more knowledge than a mere mortal, he certainly doesn't have unlimited knowledge.

39

Satan Is Not Omnipresent

Furthermore, Satan is not omnipresent, or everywhere at the same time. God is omnipresent, and wherever we go, God is there. Satan can only be at one place at one time. He does, however, give the impression of being everywhere because of a very well organized structure of demons under his control.

Satan Is Not Omnipotent

His power is limited by the will of God in the life of the believer. That truth has very dangerous implications for you if you're not a believer. If you have not made a personal commitment to Jesus Christ and are not maintaining a proper relationship with Him right now, Satan's power is essentially unlimited in your life. He can do whatever he wants. Maybe you like to think that you're the master of your destiny, the captain of your ship, but in reality, you're a puppet. Satan is pulling the strings in your life.

The Bible says in II Corinthians 4:4, "The god of this world [the devil] has blinded the eyes of them that do not believe," and that non-believers are taken captive to do Satan's will!

Have you ever noticed that most people who think they're in charge of their own lives all seem to be moving in the same direction? That's because they're following a Pied Piper, and he's whispering the same thoughts into all their minds. He's able to activate impulses inside them, and they're obeying him faithfully, all the time believing that he doesn't even exist. It's a great strategy; it has worked with brilliance and great effectiveness for centuries.

SUPERNATURAL PRESENCE

One of the devil's greatest deceptions is to make people think he doesn't exist. People envision the cartoon devil, with horns, tail, hooves and pitchfork. They laugh it off. Meanwhile, he says, "Laugh all you want. I'll see you in hell."

However, Satan's power is limited over Christians by the will of God. This is clearly illustrated in a conversation that occurred between God and Satan as recorded in the book of Job. It is a unique glimpse into the Invisible World. One day in heaven, a group of angels came before the Lord and Satan was among them. God said, "Satan, where have you been?" He said, "Just walking to and fro throughout the earth." God said, "Have you considered my servant Job? He's perfect. He's upright. He fears God and shuns evil." God was bragging about Job, just as a proud parent brags about his child. In essence, the devil said, "Let me have a few days with Job. Let me have my way in his life. Then we'll see what He's made of."

Satan said to God, "Give me some time with Job. Haven't you made a hedge of protection around him on every side?" That was accurate. God had put a hedge of protection around Job and Satan could not touch Job's person or possessions without God's permission. Of course, that is true of any believer.

We all know that God allowed tragedy to befall Job. At the same time, He knew what Job could handle; he knew his breaking point. He also knows what you can handle. He knows what your vulnerabilities are. He knows what your breaking point is.

In the upper room on the night of the last supper, Jesus leaned over and said to Simon Peter, "Satan has been asking for you by name." I think Peter started to shake in his sandals! Jesus continued, "Not only has he been asking for you by name, but he has been asking again and again that you be taken out of the care and protection of God." Now Peter was really shaking. Then Jesus said, "I've got good news for you, Simon. I have prayed for you." What confidence that must have brought to a badly shaken Simon! What confidence those words give me!

If I had to go out there and fight the devil in my own strength, I'd be completely destroyed. I'm no match for him; nor are you. We stand in the strength of God. We stand on what He has done for us at the cross. We stand in the knowledge that Jesus is praying for us. He will not let the enemy overwhelm us!

I hear a knock at the door. "Who is it?" I ask.

"It's the devil."

"Lord, would you mind getting the door?"

I'm not going to answer that door! "You get it, Lord. You know my weaknesses."

SUPERNATURAL DEFEAT

Another thing the devil doesn't want us to know is that he has been conquered at the cross of Calvary. I John 3:8 says, "For this purpose the Son of God was manifested that He might destroy the works of the devil."

What are some of this already-defeated adversary's most commonly- used strategies? It may surprise you to find that he moves in predictable patterns using the same successful tactics over and over again. I suppose he operates under the philosophy, "If it ain't broke, don't fix it." He has found these strategies have worked, so why change them?

Victor Hugo once said, "A good general must penetrate the brain of his enemy." We need to know what our enemy has in mind. II Corinthians 2:11 says, "We are not ignorant of Satan's devices." Literally, "We are not ignorant of the schemes, plans, strategies and tricks of the devil."

Satan is a dangerous wolf who often disguises himself as a sheep. Sometimes, he will come on like a lion, but more often he sneaks in like a snake. Sometimes, he appears in all of his depravity and horror. Other times, he disguises himself as an angel of light. You may be resisting him on one hand and setting up housekeeping with him on the other! When he attacked the Church in its infant stages, two primary strategies were utilized: One was blatant outward attack; the other was subtle infiltration.

Plan Number One: Frontal Attack

Satan's first thought was that by physical persecution, he could snuff out the tiny group of believers in Jerusalem. He bombarded them with harrassment and persecution and in doing so, he accomplished great things for the cause of the gospel! The Church knew that Jesus was someone worth believing in and harassment caused them to cling more tightly to each other and to God. They trusted Him for His power, and when persecution hit, they simply spread out and went everywhere preaching the Word. Instead of wrecking the church, persecution strengthened it. Much to the devil's disgust, it became a "lean, mean, preaching machine."

As Satan watched this, he realized that this tactic wasn't working, but he had an ace up his sleeve. He still had his main man —Saul of Tarsus. Saul had been responsible for the death of the first martyr of the church, a courageous young man named Stephen. Saul was out there doing the devil's bidding and Satan was clearly on a roll.

Then, things got even worse for the devil. One day, on the Damascus Road, Saul came to know Jesus Christ. He was transformed from Saul of Tarsus to Paul, the Apostle. Instead of being a man driven by hate, he became a man motivated by love and one of the most powerful preachers in the new church. What a blow to the forces of darkness! And what a victory for the kingdom of God.

Plan Number Two: Infiltration

Satan reasoned, "Hmmm...back to the drawing board. This isn't working as well as I'd hoped. I'm actually helping them." His next move was a shrewd one. He decided it was time to go undercover and infiltrate. There was a time in church history when, almost overnight, believers went from the catacombs into the palaces. This occurred when a Roman emperor known as Constantine claimed to be converted and stopped oppressing the church. Being a confessed believer himself, he elevated Christians from persecution to a place of prominence. They literally went from rags to riches, practically overnight.

The Christians' new respectability weakened them immensely. Compromise set in. Charles Colson has pointed out that history repeatedly shows us the Church either being persecuted or corrupted. This is the result of Satan's tactic of infiltration. G. Campbell Morgan said,

> "The Church persecuted has always been the Church pure. The Church patronized has always been the Church impure."

43

The devil may confront you in a blatant outward attack; maybe an enticement to do evil; maybe a temptation to become sexually permissive, to be unfaithful to your spouse, to dabble in drugs or alcohol, to steal or lie. When he uses such overt tactics, you're well aware that he's at work. "I'm not going to give in to that," you smile to yourself. So he'll come to you more subtly and say, "Let's work out a compromise. Go ahead and go to church if you want to. Go ahead and read the Bible and pray. Just lower your standards a little bit here and there. We'll get along just fine. You don't need to go to church so often, and there are other things to read besides the Bible. Take it easy. Kick back. Do it later. Mañana." Through compromise and infiltration, he can immobilize and sterilize you. Satan's infiltration of the Church has proved to be his most effective method.

Plan Number Three: Counterfeits

Jesus told the parable of a man who sowed wheat. In the night an enemy came and sowed tares among the wheat. A tare, which grows from a darnel seed, is a plant that, in its initial stages of growth, looks exactly like a stalk of wheat. Ultimately, it uproots the wheat. Satan has flooded the market with counterfeits and imitations. There are so many frauds out there that a lot of nonbelievers say, "Forget it. I don't even want to deal with it. I go to catch a plane at the airport and eight people come up to me from different religious persuasions, trying to convert me. They're all out of their minds. I don't want to hear about any of it." If that's a person's reaction, it is clear that the devil's strategy has succeeded.

By sowing tares among the wheat, he causes some people to mistakenly throw the baby out with the bath water. They don't take time to consider the truth because they're so frustrated by all the imitations. You can see how well this deception has worked.

■■■■ Satan has pretenders in the pews and predators in the pulpits.

He has a counterfeit gospel. Galatians 1:8 says,

If we or an angel from heaven should preach to you a gospel contrary to that which we have preached let him be accursed.

44

II Corinthians 11:14 says, "For even Satan disguises himself as an angel of light." It's not surprising if his servants also disguise themselves as servants of righteousness. In the last days, Satan is even going to have a counterfeit Christ who will present himself as a great leader who apparently has all the answers. This man of peace will be called the Antichrist —the coming world leader.

Plan Number Four: Doubt

Satan has been in business for a long, long time. To understand just how long, you need to go back to the first book of the Bible and take a look at Genesis 3:1-7. In this foundational chapter, we are able to examine the wiles the devil used on Adam and Eve. I think you'll notice that they are precisely the same ones he's practicing on us today.

Now the serpent was more cunning than any beast of the field which the Lord God had made. And he said to the woman, "Has God indeed said, 'You shall not eat of every tree of the Garden?'" And the woman said to the serpent, "We may eat the fruit of the tree of the garden; but of the fruit of the tree which is in the midst of the garden, God has said, 'You shall not eat it, nor shall you touch it, lest you die.'" And then the serpent said to the woman, "You will not surely die. For God knows that in the day you eat of it your eyes will be opened and you will be like God, knowing good and evil." And when the woman saw that the tree was good for food, that it was pleasant to the eyes, and a tree desirable to make one wise, she took of its fruit and ate. She also gave to her husband with her, and he ate. Then the eyes of both of them were opened, and they knew that they were naked; and they sewed fig leaves together and made themselves coverings.

Plan Number Five: Tolerance   45

Do you recognize the basic principles of satanic attack? When Satan wanted to lead the first man and woman into sin, he started by attacking the woman's mind. II Corinthians 11:3 says,

I am afraid lest as the serpent deceived Eve by his craftiness, your minds should be led astray from the simplicity and purity and devotion to Christ.

The human mind is incredibly vulnerable and impressionable. It is in the mind that we reason, contemplate and allow our imaginations free rein. That is why the Bible warns us,

The weapons of your warfare are not physical but spiritual and mighty in God for pulling down strongholds, therefore cast down imaginations and every high thing that exalts itself against the knowledge of Christ, and bring every thought into the captivity of the obedience of Christ.

When you daydream, contemplate or think about things that are harmful spiritually, you've taken the first step toward doing those things. Today, some of the things we once considered taboo and would not even speak about, are now commonly discussed; they're joked about on television sitcoms; they're made light of in print, in movies and in music. This familiarity constitutes the first step toward a change in human behavior. Public acceptance convinces us that maybe certain actions aren't so bad after all.

It's the same in our personal lives. We may not respond to some blatantly obvious temptation. If the devil were to come to you and say, "I've got a great idea! I want you to think about this: Why don't you have an affair with your secretary? Then, end your marriage in divorce and watch your children be estranged from you. Why not allow your whole life to fall apart? Ultimately, you can turn to alcohol and die prematurely. What do you think? Shall we start right away?"

Your obvious response to such a blatant approach would be, "Get serious. Do you think I'm a fool? I'd never do that." Of course, the devil knows this. So, he comes to you with a different tactic. He subtly suggests, "Wouldn't it be fun if you just dreamed a little? Of course, you'll never act on it. Just think about it. Take a trip to fantasy island." So you start thinking about it, toying with it in your imagination. Then, no longer satisfied with just fantasizing about it, you start flirting a little bit with someone other than your wife or husband. Nothing serious, of course, just an innocent lunch together. Then, one thing leads to another and the next thing you know, you're in serious trouble. You say, "How could this have happened? I can't believe I fell into such an obvious trap!" The Bible says, "Don't give a foothold to the devil." But you did.

Plan Number Six: Temptation

Temptation usually starts in the realm of our minds. It's been said, "You can't stop a bird from flying over your head, but you can stop him from building a nest in your hair." That means, I can't prevent an impure thought from passing by, but I can keep it from becoming a part of my thoughts. It's not a sin to be tempted. It's a sin to give in to the temptation.

We've all been assaulted by impure thoughts. They often come at the worst times. You may be in church, reading the Bible or singing a praise song when some devious, bizarre, sinful thought comes to your mind. Then the devil says, "How could you think such a thing? You call yourself a Christian?" It's one of the oldest tricks in his book. That's why we should bring every thought into captivity to the obedience of Christ. The next time Satan brings up that sinful thought, remind yourself, "I didn't come up with that, and I'm not going to think about it. It's evil, impure, and I don't want anything to do with it."

The Bible says in I John 2:16, "All that is in the world, the lust of the eyes, the lust of the flesh, and the pride of life is of the world."

That breaks down basically the three categories of temptation. The lust of the eyes, the lust of the flesh and the pride of life.

The lust of the eyes is mental temptation: what we see, contemplate, think about, fantasize over. Most sin begins here.

The lust of the flesh usually follows the lust of the eyes. At this stage, thoughts are translated into actions. A person who has fallen into the lust or desires of the flesh is basically a person who gives in to his impulses.

I have a dog who does pretty much whatever he wants to do. When he feels like taking a nap, he collapses. When he gets hungry, he goes and rustles up something. If he feels the urge to do something else, he does it. He just gives in to whatever his impulses are. There are people like that. They just live to gratify their cravings and their desires. They serve the lust of the flesh.

The pride of life is more subtle. You might be a person who doesn't indulge in other sinful activities. You live a moral life. You have a fine family. You work hard, with honesty, and enjoy a good career. You're pursuing excellence and knowledge. You might even be a religious person. You might be patting yourself on the back saying, "I'm so wonderful. I'm so moral. I'm so good. I'm so intelligent. Best of all, I'm so humble." You can be deceived by the pride of life. Egotism and pride are as much a deception as the lust of the flesh or the lust of the eyes.

Bearing in mind these three ideas, the lust of the eyes, the lust of the flesh, and the pride of life, let's see if we can find them in Eve's temptation in the Garden. "The woman saw the tree was pleasant to the eyes." There it is, the lust of the eyes. "She saw that it was good for food. She tasted of it." There's the lust of the flesh. "She saw it was desirable to make one wise." Finally, the pride of life.

There you have it. The enemy will hit you in those three areas over and over again.

Plan Number Seven: Deception

This passage also teaches us that one of the foundational strategies of the devil is lying. Revelation 12:9 says, "He's the serpent of old who is called the devil and Satan who deceives the whole world."

Jesus said of Satan, "There is no truth in him for he is a liar and the father of lies."

Questioning God's Word

48

We see him lying to Eve. First of all, in verse 1 he questioned God's Word. He was so cunning! "Has God indeed said you shall not eat of every tree of the garden?" Satan didn't deny that God had spoken. He simply questioned whether God had really said what Eve had thought He'd said.

He implied, "God doesn't really love you, Eve. If God really loved you, He would let you eat of any tree that appealed to you. Therefore, when He says you cannot eat of this tree, He's holding something back from you that really need to look into." He questions the Word of God. He will also do that in the life of the believer. He will say to us, "Do you really believe the Bible is the Word of God? Do you really think you're saved? You're not saved. God hasn't forgiven you. You don't deserve it. Look at you. Look at that sin you just committed. You call yourself a Christian? Don't even think of going to church. That would be the ultimate hypocrisy. Stay home and watch television instead. Don't you dare pray. God won't listen to you. Forget about reading the Bible because God will not speak to you through it anyway, after what you've done."

You say, "Thanks, devil, that's great advice."

He's a liar!

 When you sin, that's all the more reason to pray and ask God to forgive you.

When you sin, that's all the more reason to go to church and get help and support from your Christian friends.

When you sin, it's vital that you read the Word of God to see what it has to say to you. Then, act decisively on it.

Satan lies to you.

Don't base your salvation on the way you feel but on what God has said. God says in I John 5,

> These things we have written unto you that believe on the name of the Son of God, that you may KNOW that you have eternal life.

Now that's something to hang on to! Memorize that and remind yourself of it when you are going through times of struggle.

Denying God's Word

First, Satan questioned God's Word. Then he said, "You shall not die" in verse 4. It's but a short step from questioning the Word of God to denying it. If Eve had not listened to Satan questioning God's Word, she would never have fallen. That is why the Bible says, "Resist the devil and he will flee from you." It's because Eve was talking to him that she fell into his trap. Don't converse with him! Satan's lies are so subtle.

Tennyson said, "A lie that is all of a lie can be met with and fought outright. A lie that is partly the truth is a harder matter to fight." When Satan lies openly and blatantly, it's one thing, but when he mixes a little truth into his lies, discernment becomes more difficult.

Substitutions for God's Word

In verse 5 Satan says, "You shall be as gods knowing good and evil."

First, he questioned God's Word.

Second, he denied God's Word.

Third, he substitutes his own lie.

GOD'S PLAN

Eve had a choice to make. Should she believe the Word of God or believe the word of the devil? We know which choice she made and we've all been paying for it ever since. I don't mean to fault just Eve. Adam was involved, too. They both sinned and did what

God told them not to do. Eve and Adam failed to use the weapon God has given all of us to use during times of temptation. This weapon is His Word, also known as the "Sword of the Spirit."

Satan tried to deceive Jesus during His temptation in the wilderness. Satan asked, "Why don't you jump off the tip of this temple because it is written, 'He shall give His angels charge over you to protect you in all your ways.'" The devil knows the Bible, but he quoted it out of context.

Someone once saw W.C. Fields reading a Bible. Amazed, the observer said, "Why are you, W.C. Fields, reading that?" In his best form, the famous comedian replied, "Looking for loopholes.... Looking for loopholes...."

50

Satan, as a student of Scripture, does precisely the same thing. Jesus replied, "It is written, thou shalt not tempt the Lord thy God." He pulled out that sword of the spirit and—touché! That's what we need to do. We need to know the Word of God. Then, when the enemy comes with his lies and temptations and distortions, we can use scripture offensively to defend ourselves.

Maybe you're wondering, "Why does God even allow temptation? Life would be so much easier if God would take all temptation away and let us cruise on through life until we get to heaven!" Temptation, believe it or not, can have a positive impact on our lives.

> Temptation separates the men from the boys;
> the women from the girls;
> the wheat from chaff;
> the real from the false.

When you're a true child of God and you are tempted, you cling to God all the more.

A.B. Simpson said, "Temptation exercises our faith and teaches us to pray. It is like a military drill and a taste of battle to the young soldier. It puts us under fire and compels us to exercise our weapons and prove their potency. It shows us the recourse of Christ and the preciousness of the promises of God. Every victory gives us new confidence in our victorious leader and new courage for the next onslaught of the foe."

If you are not walking with the Lord, you'll probably dabble with temptation. You may toy with it. If you do, you will ultimately fall into sin. On the other hand, James 1:12 says,

> Happy is the man that endures temptation, for when
> he has been approved he will receive the crown of
> life which the Lord has promised to them that love
> Him.

When you resist temptation, you will grow stronger. Let me give you a word of warning. Temptation will often hit you during times of blessing and spiritual victory. Brace yourself. A lot of times after God has really ministered to you or has used you, Satan will have his bow loaded with his flaming arrows, and he'll nail you. Jesus was faced with his most challenging temptation apart from the Cross right after His baptism, when the Spirit of God came upon Him in the form of a dove. It was after the dove that the devil came. Jesus was also confronted by a demon-possessed person after he had been transfigured on the mountain with Moses and Elijah. It's after the blessing, that buffeting and attacks often come.

We need to keep up our guard.

51

THE INVISIBLE WORLD

CHAPTER

Satan's Tactics

Many of us have seen the classic sci-fi thriller, *The War of the Worlds*. In this chapter, we will delve into "The War of the Heavens." We've been looking at the Invisible World, the realm in which God and Satan dwell, where a supernatural battle is being fought. A war has raged there for centuries, and one day, it will come to a conclusion.

To find that grand finale, we will look at Revelation 12 where we find an overview of the battle of the ages.

> Now a great sign appeared in heaven: a woman clothed with the sun, with the moon under her feet, and on her head a garland of twelve stars. Then being with child, she cried out in labor and in pain to give birth.

> And another sign appeared in heaven: behold a great fiery red dragon having seven heads and ten horns, and seven diadems on his heads. His tail drew a third of the stars of heaven and threw them to the earth. And the dragon stood before the woman who was ready to give birth, to devour her child as soon as it was born.

> And she bore a male Child who was to rule all nations with a rod of iron. And her Child was caught up to God and to His throne. Then the woman fled into the wilderness, where she has a place prepared by God that they should feed her there one thousand two hundred and sixty days.

> And war broke out in heaven: Michael and his angels fought against the dragon; and the dragon and his angels fought, but they did not prevail, nor was a place found for them in heaven any longer. So the great dragon was cast out, that serpent of old, called the Devil and Satan, who deceives the whole

world; he was cast down to the earth, and his angels were cast out with him.

Then I heard a loud voice saying in heaven, 'Now salvation, and strength, and the kingdom of our God, and the power of His Christ have come, for the accuser of our brethren, who accused them before our God day and night, has been cast down.'

And they overcame him by the blood of the Lamb and by the word of their testimony, and they did not love their lives to the death. Therefore rejoice, O heavens and you who dwell in them! Woe to the inhabitants of the earth and the sea! For the devil has come down to you, having a great wrath because he knows that he has a short time (Revelation 12:1-12).

Part of our discussion will be about Satan's destiny. Allow me to give you a little "sneak preview." The devil and his demons are going to be bitterly defeated. Satan and his fallen angels are destined to the lake of fire, another name for hell. That is where the devil is going. He knows that.

SATAN'S TIME IS SHORT

Here in Revelation 12, however, we're given a description of a heavenly war, a spiritual battle. Read again verse 12,

Therefore rejoice, O heavens and you who dwell in them! Woe to the inhabitants of the earth and the sea! For the devil has come down to you, having a great wrath because he knows that he has a short time.

It bears repeating, Time is short. The devil knows his days are numbered. That is why, at this very moment, he is going for the jugular and pulling out all the stops, "playing his hand," if you will. He knows his judgment is rapidly approaching.

THE INVISIBLE WORLD

Satan During the Great Tribulation

The Bible describes a tribulation period, with a time frame of seven years, that is going to come on the earth when God's judgment will be poured out. During that time, Satan will play his trump card with the emergence of his unholy trinity: Satan, himself; the Antichrist and the False Prophet. Satan will empower the other two for their evil tasks.

Satan has always been an imitator, not an originator. He sees that there is a Holy Trinity comprised of a Father, Son and Holy Spirit. Satan always wanted to be God. That's why he was thrown out of heaven in the first place. He said, "I will be like God. I will sit on His throne." Satan says, "I'm going to run the show. I'll be like God. I'll give the power and authority to my own version of Jesus Christ — the Antichrist.

The prefix, *anti*, could also be translated "instead of" as well as "against." He is Satan's masquerade messiah, his counterfeit Christ. As a world leader with a charismatic personality, this antichrist figure will be accepted by most of the earth's inhabitants during the tribulation period. He will arrive with answers to the problems this world is facing and will offer solutions for world peace. When this occurs, people will hail him as the Messiah, Himself.

Working alongside this false messiah in Revelation will be another person who is identified as the False Prophet. This counterfeit Holy Spirit will perform miracles and will oversee the religious aspects of the Antichrist's kingdom.

Satan will be playing God; the Antichrist will be masquerading as the Messiah; and the False Prophet will pretend to be the Holy Spirit. Those are going to be very intense times. Angelic activity, both holy and unholy, will reach a fever pitch. The book of Revelation tells us that the fallen angels or demons will drive the world's armies into one final battle called Armageddon. There will be an outbreak of excessive violence, drug abuse and sorcery.

Angels During the Tribulation

During the tribulation period, God's holy angels will be at work too. The Scripture teaches, "When the enemy comes in like a flood, the Lord will raise up a standard against him." We see this illustrated as an angel is observed flying through the heavens with the message of the everlasting gospel. We also read of an angel warning the inhabitants of the earth not to take the mark of the beast.

Jesus said that the gospel must be preached to all men before the end comes. Based on this, some say that Jesus cannot return until we, as the church, get the gospel out to the whole world. Therefore, they maintain that we should "help" the Lord return a little sooner by aggressively sharing our faith. Naturally, we should share our faith but it isn't necessary for us to do this in order to expedite the Lord's return. The Lord could come back at any moment.

It may be that the way God is ultimately going to get the gospel to all the world is through the angels. They'll do a massive mop–up operation in areas we believers were unable to reach. The closer we get to the end, the more we'll see angels and demons hard at work. The supernatural conflict will be raging at full steam.

57

This battle will culminate with the war in heaven between none other than the Archangel, Michael, and the powerful fallen angel, Satan.

SATAN'S HISTORY

The Beginning of Hostilities

The battlelines for this conflict were laid down a long time ago in the Garden of Eden. In Genesis, we find Satan, already in his fallen state, seeking to entice man and destroy the paradise God had made for Adam and Eve. When God's condemnation reached him, he was told,

> You are cursed, and you will eat dust all the days of
> your life, and I will put enmity between you and the
> woman and between your seed and her seed. And
> He (speaking of one who was coming) will bruise
> your head but you will bruise His heel.

When I was in the sixth grade, I got into a fight with a fifth grader. He beat me up horribly. It was a very embarrassing, humiliating experience. Of course, it is completely unacceptable to be beaten up by a fifth grader when you're in the sixth grade. It doesn't matter if he's seven feet tall and a junior Mr. Universe, it just isn't done! What matters is that he's a fifth grader and you're a sixth grader. However, I can tell you from personal experience that there are exceptions to that rule.

We were scheduled to have the big fight after school. The truth of the matter is that I didn't even want to fight this guy, but he thought I'd challenged him to a fight. He said something to me and I answered, "Do you want to fight me?" I wasn't trying to challenge him; I was simply trying to determine what his intentions were, but he said, "Okay, when? After school?"

I gulped.

All the kids said, "Yeah," knowing I would be pulverized.

On the school bus, I realized I had to think fast to defuse the situation. So, I used my wits. I went over and sat with this guy and tried to make friends. I cracked a few jokes. We laughed and had a great time. I thought, *"All right, I'm not going to be pulverized after all."* I heaved a sigh of relief.

But after I got off the school bus, he was walking right behind me. All of a sudden, he yelled, "Come on, Laurie." I spun around. He jumped on me and threw me on the ground. He started pounding my head into the dirt. I heard the kids crying in unison, "Make Laurie eat dust! Make Laurie eat dust!" My pride was more wounded than anything else that day.

In the Garden of Eden, God was saying to Satan, "You're going to eat dust the rest of your life." An important thing was stated here. God said, "He will bruise your head, but you will bruise His heel."

God had Satan's attention and he probably said, "He? Who? Who are you talking about?" God in essence had just said, "There is coming One that is going to nail your hide to the wall."

"Oh yeah? We'll see about that," Satan most likely responded.

The spiritual battlelines were drawn. In the Garden of Eden, Satan learned that Someone was going to bruise him. He was forewarned, and from that moment on, Satan sought to stop that One who ultimately would come and deal the decisive blow against him.

Satan's Search for Our Savior

He was crafty, and it didn't take him many years to determine that this One would come through the Jewish race. So anti-

Semitism was born. Anti-Semitism, of course, is persecution or hatred of Jewish people. It has been with us for centuries and continues to this day. Anti–Semitism really has a satanic origin, as it inspires men and women to hate God's chosen people. Satan persecuted the Jews knowing the Messiah was coming from among them.

Satan didn't know exactly when He would appear on the scene. This was a problem for him.

- In the book of Exodus, we see Satan's persecution of the Jews through such means as Pharaoh's extermination of Jewish baby boys. At that time, God protected His chosen one by having Moses hid in a basket among the bulrushes. Phaorah's daughter found him there and God's plan moved forward.

- Later, there was Haman and his wicked plot to kill all the Jews on the gallows; this story is detailed in the book of Esther. Again, God spared His chosen people by a miracle.

- In the New Testament, we read about King Herod. In his paranoia, after hearing that a king had been born, he ordered that all Jewish boys under the age of two years be killed. He was responding to Satan's ongoing attempt to stop the Messiah. But God kept the baby Jesus safe by sending Joseph and his little family to Egypt.

59

Satan's Seeming Success

When Jesus finally came on the scene and was clearly identified, Satan masterminded the crucifixion. He entered into the heart of Judas Iscariot who betrayed the Lord for thirty pieces of silver. When Jesus was taken to the cross and spikes were driven through His hands and feet, no doubt the forces of hell gave a victory shout and thought they had won. The battle was over. Little did they know that Jesus had come for this very purpose. In all his rage and anger and hatred for God, Satan had actually helped God accomplish His own purpose. Acts 2:23 says,

> Jesus was delivered by the determined counsel and foreknowledge of God. You have taken and

crucified Him and put Him to death. You put Him
to death, but it was all according to God's plan.

I heard a story that illustrates this point. Once there was a
man who had a great estate. Toward the back of his estate, he had a
beautiful redwood forest with one tree that towered above all the
others. The man had great pride in his forest, but especially in that one
strong, towering redwood.

The man had a neighbor who burned with jealousy and envy.
Every day, that neighbor imagined ways that he could make the
man's life miserable. One day, the neighbor devised a cruel plot. He
said to himself, "I'm going over there in the night and cut down that
one prize tree. I'll chop it down and he can watch it fall."

That night, the neighbor grabbed his saw and climbed over
the fence. He frantically began to saw the massive redwood. He
hadn't realized how thick it was or how long it would take to cut it
down. Sweat poured down his face but he continued to saw, fueled by
his burning hatred. Soon, the night was almost past and dawn was
beginning to break. Still, the envious neighbor sawed. He was
exhausted but his hatred drove him on.

As dawn broke, he saw his wealthy neighbor walking toward
him accompanied by another man. He thought, "This is perfect. The
tree will fall right in front of him and he will see it done." In his frenzy
to finish, he sawed so frantically that he failed to notice which
direction the tree would fall. The tree slowly tipped over and
thundered to the ground right where that jealous man was positioned
and he was pinned beneath it's weight. Yet, even in all his pain, lying
under the heavy tree trunk, he took pride in the fact that he had cut
down his neighbor's prize tree. His joy was shortlived.

The owner stooped over him as he lay there and said, "I don't
know why you've done this, but you have helped me more than you
will ever know! This gentleman," and he pointed to his companion,
"is a builder. I've been wanting to build on this land but that big tree
has been in my way! I couldn't figure out how to cut it down. How
can I ever thank you? You've helped me accomplish my purpose!"

Not only did the jealous man help his neighbor accomplish
his purpose, but he destroyed himself in the process.

That is exactly what happened at the cross of Calvary. Satan masterminded the crucifixion and brought it all about. Little did he know that he actually enabled God to strike the decisive blow against him. Satan was judged at the cross of Calvary when Jesus died there. He defeated himself. He shot himself in the foot. Like Haman many years earlier, he hung himself on his own gallows.

SATAN'S POWER

In Revelation 12, verse 3, the dragon having seven heads and ten horns is identified as Satan. Horns in Revelation are symbols of power and authority, and this shows that he is in a position of great power. The Bible says that Satan is the god of this world. He is the prince of the power of the air. One of his most brilliant strategies has been to manipulate world events to tragic ends, and then gloat when people say, "How could a God of love allow this to happen? I thought God was supposed to be in control!" when all along it was Satan, the "god of this world," who masterminded it.

He Has Wealth

True, Satan does have considerable power at this time, but it is ultimately going to be taken away from him. In the temptation in the wilderness, Satan came to Jesus and showed Him all of the kingdoms of the world. He said, "All of these will I give to you if you will worship me."

Jesus didn't refute that statement. The reason is because it was perfectly true. Satan does possess all the kingdoms of the world, and he actually was offering them to Jesus at that moment in return for Jesus worshipping him as God.

He Has Influence

In verse four, we read that Satan took with him a third of the stars of heaven, and those stars are later identified as angels. Do you want to read about the real "Star Wars?" Here it is: the angels were fighting. When Satan was first thrown out of heaven, he took one–third of the angels with him. As mentioned, the Bible tells us there are millions of angels so if Satan took a third of them, he has a sizable force.

How did he do it? Maybe he did it the same way that he deceives us—through his lies. The Bible identifies him as the father of lies. Perhaps he lied to those angels to get them to follow him and they didn't realize that he was leading them into a fiery judgment. He's still using the same kind of deception to entice many people today. He tells them whatever lie is necessary in order to destroy their lives.

He Has Position

We read in Revelation 12:7-8 that:

> War broke out in heaven. Michael and his angels fought with the dragon, and the dragon and his angels did not prevail, nor was there found a place for them in heaven any longer.

It's amazing to think that there was a time when Michael and Lucifer were on the same side. Now they are antagonists, fighting against each other. Satan was once a high-ranking angel. It is possible, though it is not clearly spelled out, that he may even have held a rank equal to that of Michael. Perhaps he was an archangel. Whatever his rank was, we know he was a powerful angel in heaven and he is now a tremendously powerful fallen angel on earth.

SATAN USES HIS POWER AGAINST US

Satan Accuses Us Before God

One of the names of Satan is "the accuser of the brethren." We read this in Revelation 12, verse 10. One of Satan's primary weapons against believers is accusation. He accuses us before God.

There's a dramatic story in the Bible that illustrates this quite well. It's recorded in Zechariah 3. We read,

> He showed me Joshua, the high priest standing before the angel of the Lord, and Satan standing at his right hand to oppose him. And the Lord said to Satan, "The Lord rebuke you, Satan, Indeed the Lord who has chosen Jerusalem rebuke you! Is this not a brand plucked from the fire?"

This is a vivid portrait: Joshua, the high priest, is standing before God. Satan is at his right hand, accusing him.

The devil is still using the tactic of accusation to great effect. Look how subtle he is. Before we sin, he tempts us, "You can get away with this. No one will ever know. I promise not to tell, if you won't." However, if you sin, he says, "You'll never get away with this. You're never going to pull this one off." First, he entices you and afterward, he condemns you.

Satan's Accusations Are True

I firmly believe, as a pastor, that the church should not be a museum for saints, but a hospital for sinners. If you're made of the same fiber that I am, then you're a sinner. You need help and forgiveness on a regular basis. I need to be forgiven every single day and you do too. Thank God we can go to church and be encouraged by one another.

63

The last thing we should do is sit in judgment of each other. We should be ready to help our wounded brothers and sisters. Next week it may be you! You may come staggering in with the flaming arrows of the wicked one embedded in your chest. The Bible doesn't teach believers to push those arrows from hell in even further. Rather, "If you see a brother overtaken in a fault, restore such a one with a spirit of meekness lest you also be tempted."

The way some Christians react to others who have fallen, you would think the Scripture said, "If you see a brother overtaken in a fault, finish him off! Make sure you gossip about him and have a condescending attitude toward him!"

The opposite is true. We Christians, all living in the same world, need each other and we need to hold each other up because "our adversary, the devil, is a roaring lion walking about seeking whom he may devour."

Warren Wiersbe, in his insightful book, "The Strategy of Satan," explains that when Satan talks to you about God, he lies. When he talks to God about you, he tells the truth. When you fall in sin, he keeps track.

He may say: "Did you see what King David just did? He's supposed to be a man after Your own heart, right? Well, he just committed adultery. Not only did he commit adultery, he committed murder to cover up his sin of adultery. Did you see that? Judge him!"

"God! Did you see that your disciple Peter just denied you openly, not once, not even twice, but three times? Are you going to let him get away with that?"

That's what he's doing right now. At this very moment he might be bringing your name up before God, standing in His presence and accusing you.

GOD USES HIS POWER TO SAVE US

Accusations Aren't Conviction

It is important that we learn to distinguish between Satan's accusations and the Holy Spirit's conviction. Sometimes, when Satan is accusing us and condemning us, we think it's the Spirit of God. I've met people that say, "I could never ask God to forgive me. I feel so guilty." They think God's driving them away when it's really Satan's doing.

A feeling of guilt and shame is not necessarily a bad thing if it comes from the Spirit of God. Guilt can become our friend, our ally, to bring us back to God. If it drives us into despair and hopelessness, we're listening to the wrong voice. If it drives us to our knees before God to ask for forgiveness, it's good.

Some psychologists tell us that guilt is never good, but I think a lot of us could use a good dose of old fashioned guilt. We feel it because we are guilty of sin! When we sin, it's appropriate to feel remorse and to be sorry. If you don't feel sorry for what you've done, you'll go out and do it again. The Bible says that godly sorrow produces repentance.

Remorse Isn't Repentance

Some people can blubber up a story. "Oh, I'm so sorry." What they really mean is, "I'm so sorry I got caught. Next time I'll be more careful."

Warren Wiersbe also reminds us that true sorrow is positive when there is a deep sense of regret that can drive you to back to God.

If it drives you away from God, making you feel condemned, it is from Satan himself.

When the Spirit of God convicts you, He uses the Word of God in love and seeks to bring you back into fellowship with your Heavenly Father.

- When Satan accuses you, he uses your own sins in a hateful way and seeks to make you feel helpless and hopeless.

- The Spirit of God, when He points out our sin, will do it in order to bring us to Christ.
- Satan will use our sin to drive us away from Christ.
- Anytime we feel we can't go to God, we're listening to the devil.

Don't listen to him! He's an accuser and a liar and he's out to get you.

Chastening Isn't Punishment

The Bible says whom the Lord loves He chastens. God loves you so much that when you stray, He's going to make it difficult for you. He's going to convict you. You're going to sense an uneasiness when you start something you know you shouldn't do. Don't resent that feeling. Thank God that it's there.

Conscience Can't Be Trusted

The time to worry is when you're sinning and you don't feel any remorse or guilt. Suppose you're sexually involved with your boyfriend or girlfriend or some man or woman to whom you are not married. At first, you were flooded with a sense of conviction and guilt but as you repeat your sin, you begin to rationalize. In your own thinking, distorted by sin, you decide it must be okay. "I don't feel guilty. I still go to church and read the Bible. Then, I sleep with my girlfriend. God must approve."

It is surprising how many people fall into that pattern. "God hasn't done anything to me. He must not be too angry," you reason. If you think this way, you're being misled by the illusive glamour and trickery of sin. The Bible says, "Because sentence is not executed quickly, the hearts of the sons of man are set to do evil." In other words, since you haven't yet been nailed for what you've done, you think you never will. That's a very loose paraphrase, but that's what the passage says.

Don't be fooled. If you're sinning, God is displeased. The Bible clearly teaches, "Be not deceived, God is not mocked. Whatsoever a man sows, that shall he also reap." Moses' warning to Israel still holds true today: "Be sure your sin will find you out." If you continue to do something the Bible says is wrong without a sense of remorse it only means that your heart is growing hard and your conscience is being seared with a hot iron.

Repentance is Required

If you can even faintly hear the Spirit of God speaking to you, repent and come back and ask God to forgive you before you go too far. People ask me, "Can you sin so much God will not forgive you?" No. There's always hope. There is no "point of no return" but you can sin so much that you will not want to be forgiven. God will always offer the lifeline to you. He'll always reach out to save you.

Nonetheless, you must call on the name of the Lord to be saved. If you keep sinning and running from Him, there could come a point at which your conscience becomes so seared and your heart so hard that you won't want His forgiveness any more. Then you will have gone too far.

Forgiveness Is Waiting

Our sole defense against the devil's accusation is the intercession of Jesus on our behalf. What am I going to say when the devil says, "Did you see what Greg Laurie just did?" Everything he said may be true!

Some may rationalize their sins with excuses like, "Well, I can explain everything. It's the woman you gave me. It's not my fault." Adam already tried that one. God didn't buy it!

"That girl tempted me. It's not my fault." "That guy was coming on strong. I couldn't resist. I'm not responsible." "That guy cut me off on the freeway. That's why I rammed him. He deserved it!" Whatever reasons you offer, they are in reality only lame excuses that won't hold water. If you've gotten yourself into sin, it's because you made a choice to do it.

Salvation Is Complete

Our only defense is the fact that Jesus is sticking up for us, standing in the gap, and interceding.

Let's go back to the courtroom scene, only now I am the one standing before God instead of Joshua. Jesus is my defense attorney. Satan is standing at my right hand as a prosecuting attorney, reading off the list of grievances and broken laws. Sitting on the bench is God, Himself.

Satan steps forward and says to the judge, "I would like to read the following accusations against Greg Laurie. Do you have a couple of years?" He reads one after another. He starts with my childhood. He brings up things I've forgotten all about. On he goes through my teenage years and into my adult life.

My heart sinks. I listen and bury my face in my hands and think, "I'm done for! They're going to lock me up and throw away the key."

Then, I look over at my defense attorney, Jesus. He's sitting there as calm as can be. Shouldn't He be taking notes? Finally, after what seems like an eternity, Satan completes his accusations and rests his case.

Jesus stands up. What could He possibly say about me that could counteract all the bad things I've done? Quietly, Jesus walks up to the bench (unusual in a courtroom where there is great respect for decorum). He leans forward and I overhear Him say to the judge, "Dad, we both know that Greg is guilty of all the things he's been accused of. We also know that I paid the price for his sins when I died on the cross."

The judge lifts up His gavel and pounds it on the stand, saying, "Case dismissed. All is forgiven."

The only reason I'm forgiven is because of Jesus. This is only true because of what He's done for me, not because of what I've done for Him. I could never be forgiven because of anything I've accomplished for Him. I'm declared "free of sin" only because Jesus died for me on the cross of Calvary. Jesus said to Peter, "Satan has been asking that you be taken out of God's protection, but I have prayed for you."

67

That is my defense against the accusations of Satan. Jesus is standing up for me; He's standing in the gap for me.

I John 2:1 says, "My little children, I'm writing these things unto you that you may not sin, and if any sins, we have an advocate with the Father who is Jesus Christ the righteous."

Victory Is Ours

How did the believers in Revelation 12 overcome Satan? Verse 11 says, "They overcame him by the blood of the Lamb, by the word of their testimony, and they did not love their lives to the death."

Suffice it to say that Satan can be overcome. How? By the blood of the Lamb. At the cross, Christ Jesus struck the final, decisive blow against Satan and his forces. It's through the blood of the Lamb we can approach God and find the help that we need.

Satan says, "You can't come to Christ. God will never forgive you. You've committed the unpardonable sin." He's a liar, trying to keep you from God who wants to forgive you.

Ephesians 2:13 says, "You who used to be far off had been made near by the blood of Jesus Christ."

You say, "God would never receive me." You're wrong; He will!

Jesus says, "Whoever will come unto me I will not cast them out." That means that He will receive every man and woman, no matter what crime they have committed, and He will give them His forgiveness through the shed blood.

Jesus is the Only Way

Because Jesus shed His blood on the cross of Calvary, we can come to know God. On the other hand, if you think that living a good life or being moral or religious will make you acceptable to God, you're in for a big surprise. Apart from trusting Jesus, there's nothing you or I can do about sin.

The Bible says, "There is no other name given under heaven whereby a man can be saved." There is no other way to reach God. Jesus' cross is the only bridge into heaven.

CHAPTER

*Three Steps To
Victory*

Many believers are shocked to find out that the Christian life is not ...

a playground

but a battleground.

It's not a life of ease,

 but a life of conflict, warfare and opposition.

The good news is that we're in the right army! Before we knew Christ, we were opposing God. Our fight was with the Creator, and we were lined up on the wrong side of the battle. Now that we've received Christ, we are on the right side.

I remember when I first heard the gospel at the age of seventeen. I was told that I was either for Jesus or against Him. Looking around at a group of truly committed high school believers, I realized they were clearly for Him and I was acutely aware that I was on the wrong side of the fence. I wanted to rectify that immediately, which I did. Today, I'm no longer fighting against God; I'm fighting alongside Him.

Do you remember the story of Jacob? He wrestled with the Angel of the Lord at a place called Peniel, and afterward he said, "I saw God face–to–face"(Genesis 32:30). In the beginning Jacob was wrestling with God, and in the end he surrendered to God. At that point, God changed his name from Jacob, which means "deceiver and heel catcher," to Israel, which means "one who rules with God." That's the whole idea.

Before we knew God, we were fighting against Him, but now, if we've surrendered our lives to Jesus Christ, we are ruling with Him. Like Jacob (who became Israel), we now have joined His team. We have enlisted in His army and our common enemy is the devil. It has been said that you can tell a lot about a man by who his enemies are. Considering that, Satan is firmly opposed to this desire we have to walk with God. Satan is raging because he has lost some of his own, and he is incensed that we are now marching forward with God; not only seeking to hold our own ground but to gain ground for His Kingdom.

The great nineteenth century preacher, C. H. Spurgeon used to say, "You don't need to kick a dead horse." If you aren't moving anywhere in your spiritual life and are not making a difference, the devil doesn't really need to do a whole lot with you. If you are already immobilized, he will just leave you alone. However, when you get up and start moving forward, you become a direct threat to him and his kingdom.

As we've already learned, Satan uses accusation as one of his favorite tactics against us and, beyond our own efforts at employing our armor, the strongest defense we have against his accusations is the intercession of Jesus. While it is true that the devil stands at our right hand accusing us before God, it is also true that Jesus stands at the right hand of God, interceding for us. It is because of Jesus' commitment to us that we are able to succeed on the spiritual battlefield.

We are not survivors because of our great valor, our courage or our bravery, but because Jesus prays for us. You have often heard it said, "But for the grace of God, there go I." There is great truth in that statement. I stand today, because of His intercession on my behalf. Satan will accuse, but Jesus will intercede.

WE HAVE NO STRENGTH WITHOUT HIM

This brings us to an essential truth regarding spiritual warfare. To fail to understand this will spell certain defeat. Ephesians 6, verse 10 commands us,

> "Finally, my brethren, be strong in the Lord and in
> the power of His might."

Be strong in the Lord. Don't try to stand in your own strength. You and I will always fail. We must stand in His strength, recognizing that Jesus has dealt the decisive blow against Satan and his demonic forces on the Cross at Calvary. It bears repeating: When Jesus uttered those three words, "It is finished," the future course of humanity was changed. Now when people come into the protection of God, they are truly protected.

Jesus said, "No one will pluck you out of My hand. He whom the Son sets free is free indeed"(John 10:28). The Scripture says that the non-believing world lies in the power of the wicked one, but Satan cannot touch us when we are in Christ. While it is true that Satan is a roaring lion seeking to devour us, he can only roar and snarl. He can't really get hold of us and take us away from the Lord. However, if we yield to Satan, that's quite another matter.

The Bible says, "To whom you yield yourself servants to obey, his servant you are." Whether I yield to sin or to righteousness, it is a choice I make. If I yield to Satan's temptations and enticements, I can become entrapped, but if I choose not to yield to him, to keep my distance and resist him, the Bible tells me that "he will flee from me." Since Jesus dealt the decisive blow against Satan at Calvary, we do not have to fight for victory. Instead, we are fighting from a position of victory.

The story of David and Goliath illustrates this. That nine-foot, six-inch Philistine named Goliath taunted the men of Israel day in and day out. He was looking for a man with enough courage to fight him. No one dared to volunteer until the little shepherd boy, David, came in, running an errand for his father. David took one look at that oversized, uncircumcised Philistine and decided it was time for someone to stand up for the Lord. A deal was struck: If Goliath prevailed against David, that meant the Philistines would prevail over Israel. If David defeated Goliath, then Israel would be victorious.

So, David, the champion, advocate and representative of Israel, went into the valley with his small sling and his mighty faith in God, and he killed Goliath; therefore, because of David's heroic example, Israel found the courage to defeat the Philistines. The Israelites shared in David's victory. Because David won, they won.

In the same way, Jesus is our advocate, our representative, our champion! As David faced Goliath, Jesus faced Satan and went to the Cross, dealing the decisive blow against the devil and his forces. Now, we have a part in His victory. We don't have to go out and undertake our own conquests. From the group of believers mentioned in Revelation 12:10-11, we receive three keys for overcoming Satan.

> The accuser of the brethren was cast down, which
> accused them before God day and night and they
> overcame him by the blood of the Lamb, and by the

word of their testimony, and they loved not their
lives unto death.

WE HAVE NO FORGIVENESS WITHOUT HIM

What were the three principles these victorious saints used to
overcome Satan?

█████ The blood of the Lamb,

█████ the word of their testimony,

█████ and the fact that they loved not their lives unto death.

We can take those same three principles and apply them to
the spiritual battle we're engaged in every day. We begin our
confrontation with one simple recognition: The one reason that our
sin is forgiven, and we have access to God is because Jesus shed His
blood for us.

Hebrews 10:19 says we can have boldness to enter into the
Holy of Holies by the blood of Jesus. It is the only means of entry. So,
the next time the devil comes to you and says, "Hey, you can't pray.
God won't listen to you. You're not worthy. You don't deserve it."
You can say, "You're right. But I have access to God anyway, because
of the blood of the Lamb."

In the Old Testament, we learn about the nation of Israel
during the time they were being held in slavery, captives in Egypt.
One day, God informed His people that judgment was coming upon
the Egyptians and that He was going to slay Egypt's firstborn sons.
He instructed the Jews to kill a lamb, take its blood and apply it to
their door posts. He said, "When I see the blood, I will pass over you."
If the children of Israel obeyed, their own firstborn sons would be
spared. They could have said, "That's a great idea! Let's slay a lamb,
but we're too busy to apply the blood." If that had been the case, they
would have faced judgment as surely as any Egyptian who had not
shed a lamb's blood at all.

The principle remains the same today. I can know that Jesus'
blood was shed for me, but until I personally apply it to my own life,
it will do me absolutely no good. By that, I mean that we must
acknowledge our sin, repent of it and ask Him to forgive us since His

73

blood was shed on our behalf. We have to accept the truth, then put it into practice by believing it enough to act on it. First of all, we overcome Satan by the blood of the Lamb.

WE HAVE NO VICTORY WITHOUT HIM

Secondly, we defeat Satan by the word of our testimony. You see, it was not enough for these believers to stop Satan's control over their own lives. They wanted to attack other strongholds and win the world to Christ! Sports lovers know the principle well: The best defense is a good offense. Too many of us are just trying to hold ground when we should be gaining ground. Don't wonder, "What's the devil up to?" Redirect your thinking and instead consider, "What am I going to do next? What is God directing me to do? What's my plan?"

In a book entitled, *The Civil War*, Geoffrey C. Ward tells a story of General Grant and his adversary, General Lee, that illustrates the attitude we should have:

Right in the middle of the Battle of the Wilderness, all the staff men who'd been fighting in the East all this time—Grant had just come from the West— kept talking, "Bobbie Lee, Bobby Lee, he'll do this, that, and the other." And Grant finally told them, "I'm tired of hearing about Bobby Lee. You'd think he was going to do a double somersault and land in our rear. Quit thinking about what he's going to do to you and think about what you're going to do to him."

In the same way, we should go forward with our own sense of resolve and keep him guessing. Let Satan be the one that's defending and scrambling and trying to withstand us as we move in God's power and in His will. We shouldn't be sitting around wondering what he is plotting to do in our lives. It is foxhole mentality if we are trembling within ourselves and thinking, "I hope I make it. I hope I survive." Get up! Don't just talk about surviving, talk about conquering!

WE HAVE NO PURPOSE WITHOUT HIM

Lastly, those Revelation saints "loved not their lives to the death." That simply means they recognized that their lives belonged to God. The ultimate that Satan can hang over our heads is, "I'll kill you." The threat of losing our lives may be frightening to many of us but there are believers all over the world who face persecution at this level on a daily basis. Even in the United States, we may be persecuted although not necessarily to the degree that many others are. Around the globe men and women have been martyred for their faith throughout history. It continues to be true, even in this present day.

There aren't many people who are willing to pull out all the stops nowadays, but there are some. I remember reading about some young men who did. Their stories are recorded in a book called, *Through Gates of Splendor*, written by Elizabeth Elliot. Back in the 1950's, five young men felt God's Spirit directing them to a tribe of Equadorian natives known as the Auca Indians. This tribe was notorious for their blood–thirstiness. They had killed other foreigners who had approached them, so this was a dangerous assignment. Nevertheless, these five young men and their wives felt the call of God. They prepared, to learn the culture and customs of the Aucas and to study their language. They prayed about the right time to go.

They could have sought promising careers. They were successful in their college courses; each one had a great future ahead of him. However, they believed God had called them to invest their lives in His kingdom. So, they became missionaries and threw themselves into God's work in Ecuador. They waited for the day of His choosing.

One of those men was Nate Saint, a skilled pilot who had worked with Mission Aviation Fellowship. He devised a clever way of communicating with the Aucas. He dropped a long cable out of his plane with a bucket on the end. As he flew in circles, the bucket would dangle in one spot, hanging at the end of the line. The missionaries were able to drop gifts to the Aucas. They dropped a model airplane for them, along with pocket knives and other items. Pretty soon the Aucas were receiving the presents and putting their own gifts into the bucket in response. This was exciting because no one had been successful in establishing contact with these people before.

As the American missionaries flew over the Indian villages, the Indians waved to them. They were encouraged to think, "The time is coming when we will be able to meet these people and preach the gospel to them." They waited and waited and finally decided it was time to go. They recognized that they might lose their lives in the process, but they were fully prepared to take that chance. In his journal, Jim Elliot penned these words: "He is no fool to give up that which he cannot keep, to gain that which he cannot lose."

Jim gave a literal interpretation to the words of Jesus when He said, "If you lose your life for My sake, you will find it."

So it was that Jim Elliot, Nate Saint and the others made their trip into Auca territory. Their wives waited by the radio, anxiously listening for word. The few people who shared their secret mission were praying for them, but hours passed beyond the appointed radio contact and they heard nothing. Too much time went by.

At last a plane was dispatched, searching for the five men. The remains of the plane was sighted, the skin torn off its wings. A search party found all five of these young men slain. Every one of them had been murdered by the Aucas. To the searchers' horror, they found a lance in Jim Elliot with a gospel tract wrapped around it. It was a great tragedy.

Life magazine sent a man out to report on this act of martyrdom and courage. It gained worldwide attention, and God used the lives of these men to inspire thousands of people. Many men and women made commitments to serve Christ because of their total sacrifice.

Elizabeth Elliot had the incredible courage to go back to those same primitive Auca Indians and to share the love of Jesus Christ with them. Many of the Aucas came to know Christ, including the one that was responsible for killing her husband. Remember, "They loved not their lives, even to death."

In light of such heroes, should you stand at your post? Your mother probably told you, "Sit up straight, you have bad posture." God is saying, "Stand up straight. Quit slouching. Pay attention. Don't give up your position."

We Need Total Commitment to God

Doubt or paralyzing fear inspired by the enemy will sap your will and strength, if you let it. There is no room for cowards on the spiritual battlefield. Stand up! If your Christian life feels like drudgery; if worship with God's people or study of His Word is something you have to force yourself to do, you're already defeated. You're not standing, you're staggering; you're slouching; you have to be held up by other people. If you're giving only the least effort required of you, your mind is divided. You are halfhearted, uncertain in your whole attitude.

"Be strong" Paul says, "in the Lord." Then, he goes on to say, "Put on the armor of God." There is a balance here.

No matter how great your physique is,

how well–built you are,

how strong you are,

you can't go out on the battlefield without your armor.

If you do, the enemy's sword is going to pierce your muscular body just as quickly as it would pierce the skin of an anemic, scrawny fellow.

We Need Confidence in God

On the other hand, you'd better be strong enough to wear the armor! Without the whole armor of God, we are self-confident and we fail to take the necessary precautions against spiritual attack. Without our armor, we are vulnerable to a "spiritual Pearl Harbor." We are inclined to drop our guard. We think, "It won't happen to me. I'd never fall to that sin. I'm too strong."

I've heard it said that unguarded strength is a double weakness. Sometimes, the area where you never expect to fall is where you will be hit. This happens because, when you become self-confident, the enemy says, "We'll just see about that."

We think, "Oh, I can handle this." We don't even think about trusting God. "It's okay Lord, I'll take this on my own. No problem." We can never safely lower our guard in any area of our lives, especially in the areas where we think we're the strongest.

Remember Simon Peter's bold response after Jesus said, "One of you is going to deny Me." Peter said (allow me to embellish a bit), "I just want to get this straight right now, Lord —it won't be me. The rest of them may deny You, but I, Simon Peter, am a rock! I will never deny You."

Jesus said, "Well, Rock, let Me tell you something—before the cock crows twice, you will have denied Me three times." These are Simon Peter's famous last words: "It won't happen. Not me. Never!" Peter was self-confident, toying with sin, thinking he could handle it. The Bible says in I Corinthians 10, "Let him that thinks he stands, take heed lest he fall."

78 We Need Constant Vigil Against Sin

The same was true of King David. He was taking some leisure time, a little "R & R." We read that his troops were on the battlefield, but David was taking some time off. There is absolutely nothing wrong with taking time off. The problem is that you can never take a vacation from spiritual warfare. There are no furloughs granted. There may be a break while the enemy is regrouping, but he'll be back. You can't lower your guard and say, "I'm leaving, I just can't handle it anymore." The battle is always raging on. There, in a moment of leisure, David was more vulnerable than he ever imagined.

Alan Redpath said, "Moments of leisure are to be more dreaded than those of the most strenuous toil."

David was strolling around on the housetop when he saw a beautiful young woman bathing herself. We always point out that David sinned, and clearly he did, but that is not to say that Bathsheba did not strategically position herself within David's view. I don't know for sure, but maybe she intentionally went there. Nevertheless, if David had been engaged in the battle where he belonged instead of taking "R & R" on the rooftop, he would never have faced that particular temptation.

You know the rest of the story, how one thing led to another, and David and Bathsheba committed adultery. The fact is, David lowered his guard and he was hit.

We Need To Keep Our Eyes on Jesus

Another time for extreme caution is when we are feeling on top of the world spiritually. Some of the most concentrated demonic attacks come after we are flushed with victory or with the thrill of some spiritual experience. This is why we have to wear the whole armor of God and never go to sleep on duty. As God's soldiers, we are not left to our own devices. He has shown us what to do, what to wear, how to wear it, when to use it, and how to use it. All things that pertain to life and godliness have been provided for us. Let's stand up and be strong in the Lord.

Don't be overwhelmed by the power of your enemy or your circumstances. Don't start looking at yourself, saying, "What if this happens, or what if that happens? How am I going to handle it?" God is with you and He knows what is coming. You don't know what tomorrow holds but you know who holds tomorrow, and He has promised never to leave you or forsake you. Martin Loyd Jones said, "The moment Satan gets us to turn in on ourselves, he has plunged us into a vortex, in which we go around and around and become defeated and utterly useless as Christians." That is why it is essential that we take our eyes off ourselves and fix them on the Lord. That is why we must put on the complete armor of God.

CHAPTER

God's Battleplan

Knowing the critical strategic period of time, it is time for us to wake out of our sleep, for now is our salvation nearer than when we believed. The night is far spent, the day is at hand, let us therefore cast off, once and for all the works of darkness and put on the armor of light (Romans 13:11-12).

These alarming words were written to Christian believers. They are an exhortation informing us that it's time to shake off our lethargy and wake up from our apathy, because the night is far spent. In other words, the day is at hand, the day of the coming of the Lord. It's time for us to throw off once and for all the works of darkness and put on the armor of light!

It is clear from this passage, as well as several others, that we are living in a critical, strategic period of time. We have already pointed out that the devil is affectively utilizing his strategies in these days, and we need to have clear tactics of our own. Every battle counts, every day is important.

We've already determined that two of Satan's key attack modes entail the use of lies and accusations. Lies, because the Devil is "the father of lies," and accusations, because he is "the accuser of the brethren."

So what are we to do? Ephesians 6 reminds us,

"Finally, be strong in the Lord, and in His mighty power. Put on the full armor of God so that you can take your stand against the devil's schemes. For our struggle is not against flesh and blood, but against the rulers, against the authorities, against the powers of this dark world and against the spiritual forces of evil in the heavenly realms. Therefore put on the full armor of God, so that when the day of evil comes, you may be able to stand your ground, and after you have done everything, to stand. Stand firm then, with the belt of truth buckled around your waist, with the breastplate of righteousness in place, and with your feet fitted with the readiness that comes from the gospel of peace. In addition to all this, take up the shield of faith, with which you can extinguish all the flaming arrows of the evil one. Take the helmet of salvation and the sword of the Spirit, which is the Word of God" (Ephesians 6: 10-17).

We've been examining the "Invisible World" of the supernatural. Now, we will address the "invisible armor" that is very real and much needed as we engage in spiritual conflict. Let's consider some of the particular pieces of armor that God has developed to repulse these attacks of lies and accusations. It is essential as we examine each item of spiritual armor, that we implement all of these principles together. We must take "the whole counsel of God" and put it into practice. If we go through this armor and pick and choose only what we think we need we will most certainly go into battle ill-prepared.

What if you put on your helmet, your breastplate, and your shield but carried no sword? You'll find yourself in the unfortunate position of defending yourself or holding your ground but being unable to move forward because you have no offensive weapon. Or suppose you have your sandals on, and your belt and your sword, but as you attack the enemy's strongholds, you quickly lose what you've gained because of improper defense.

The armor Paul lays out is designed for offense and defense alike. As any observer of conflict knows, both aspects are equally important. Paul did not introduce us to the various pieces of armor in a haphazard fashion, or just as they came into his mind. They were presented under the inspiration of the Holy Spirit in the proper order, with the significance of each piece well in mind. In essence, Paul was building a case, and each article of armor leads to his final conclusion.

THE FULL ARMOR OF GOD

The armor that Paul describes consists of six pieces. The first three, which we are going to examine in this chapter, are:

- the belt of truth,
- the breastplate of righteousness, and
- the sandals of the gospel of peace.

83

These pieces were for long range preparation and protection. They were never taken off at any time. The last three pieces, which we'll consider later, are:

- the shield of faith,
- the helmet of salvation, and
- the sword of the Spirit.

These were kept in readiness, to be used when actual fighting began.

THE BELT OF TRUTH

Paul began his inventory in Ephesians 6, verse 14, saying,"Stand, therefore, having girded your waist with truth."

The Roman soldier wore a belt that bound together his loose garments, his robe and his toga. When he was relaxing, he loosened the belt. When he was poised for action, ready to engage in a contest, he "girded himself"; in other words, he "tightened his belt." Obviously, when Rome's soldiers went into combat, they didn't want to be tripping over their robes!

We could compare this with a woman running a 10k marathon in a formal gown. I've seen businesswomen in New York utilizing this principle in the way they are dressed as they make their way to work. They wear their tailored business clothes, but on their feet you find running shoes (they carry their dress shoes in an extra bag). This gives them the ability to move quickly, no doubt allowing them to dodge New York cabs and outrun muggers!

The belt was important because of two other strategic items that it held in place. The soldier's breastplate was attached to it as well as the sheath for his sword, two vital pieces of armor. If the enemy removed your belt, your garments would drop, eliminating you from action. Your breastplate would be unloosed and you'd lose the sheath for your sword. No matter how well trained you were, if your belt fell off, you were in big trouble.

Although the belt is not as dramatic as some of the other pieces of armor Paul mentions, it is indispensable. It is noteworthy that Paul begins with this particular piece of armor, because it is central to the Christian life. Let's reflect on a few other verses that relate to this concept of "tightening our belts".

Prepared For Action

Moses told Israel, concerning the eating of the Passover meal,

"You shall eat it in this manner, with your loins girded (your belt tightened), your sandals on your feet, and your staff in your hand, you shall eat it in haste."

The children of Israel were to eat the Passover meal poised for action, ready to go, in anticipation of God's impending orders to move.

In a similar vein, concerning His Second Coming, Jesus told us to be dressed in readiness, which also was translated " have your loins girded." (Luke 12:35).

Peter uses the same expression when he says, "gird up the loins of your mind."

To gird up our loins, or to tighten our belts, means that we Christians always ought to be prepared for action.

We need to be alert.
We need to be on guard.

Cliff Barrows, songleader and longtime associate of Billy Graham, once told me that his father always used to say, "Son, keep your powder dry." In other words, Cliff's father was reminding him of the Revolutionary War soldiers who needed to keep their gunpowder dry for use with their muskets. They never knew when they might be called into action. Spiritually speaking, we need to "keep our powder dry." We should never be in a position where we're not ready to move out at a moment's notice. Paul wrote to Timothy and he said, "Be instant in season and out of season"(II Timothy 4:2).

Another way to translate it is, "Be on duty at all times."

Prepared For The Coming of Christ

What does all this mean to us? For what are we to be alert ? One thing that we need to be alert for is the coming of the Lord. Jesus said,

> "Watch and be ready, for the Son of man is coming
> in an hour that you think not."

Every so often, someone will come along who claims to know exactly when Jesus will return to this earth. Somehow, they feel that they are the exception to Jesus' statement, "No man knows the day nor the hour..." Jesus said we won't know the exact time, but He did say, "of the times and the seasons you will know." As we see events occurring that fulfill certain prophecies, it causes us to be all the more alert.

Prepared For The Enemy Of Our Souls

Do you remember the incident when God dramatically reduced the size of Gideon's army? At God's instructions, Gideon admonished his soldiers, "If you are fearful and afraid, go home!" He immediately lost 22,000 men. But God had one more test for the 10,000 soldiers who remained. He said, "Tell them to drink." The men ran frantically toward a little brook of water. It was hot and they were tired, so many of the men just plunged into the water, drinking without any concern for what was going on around them. They lost sight of the danger that the enemy might be poised to ambush them there.

Out of 10,000 warriors, there were only 300 alert men who kept an eye on their surroundings, drawing the water up to their mouth as they watched. God said, "With these 300, I will save you." Here's the point God was making: "I am looking for alert men and women who are watching and ready." We must be that way! If we have tightened our belts, we are watching. We are ready. We are on call. We are always available to God.

Prepared For Reality

There's more. Paul said we are to be ready with the truth. We aren't merely to be ready in a general sense. We are always to be poised for action, specifically prepared with truth. This belt of truth, this part of the armor, is essential. Other pieces of armor are dependent upon it. This tells us that truth is the first thing we must put on. Without it, we are completely unprepared.

Exactly what does Paul mean by *truth*? He means we must have a firm conviction in our heart with regard to the facts. No uncertainties, no doubts, no lack of clarity. Satan, "the father of lies," will try to confuse us. We need to know what is true. We need to know what God has really said to us.

Eve made two mistakes in the garden of Eden.

Number one: God told her to stay away from the tree of the knowledge of good and evil, and yet, we find her standing right next to it.

Number two: She engaged in conversation with the devil.

The Bible says, "Resist the devil and he will flee from you" (James 4:7).

Eve conversed with the devil and she ended up believing the words of Satan instead of the Word of God, Who is Truth.

God's Word tells us "Thy Word is Truth..." Yet how much time do we spend looking into the Word of God? Often we wonder why our faith is weak and why our minds are so often filled with doubts. Could it be because we are listening to the wrong voices? When we don't give sufficient time to the truth of the Scriptures, we don't know fact from fiction. In Timothy 4:1, the Spirit explicitly states that in the last days some will "fall from the faith, paying attention to deceitful spirits and doctrines of demons." We have to be careful.

Look for Truth Constantly

How do we defeat these things?

■ By being ready with the truth, and

■ By girding up our lives with the truth.

Failing to do so can produce defeat before we ever have the opportunity to put on the rest of our armor. Ruth Graham, the wife of Evangelist Billy Graham, has written a book called, *Legacy of a Pack Rat*. It is collection of stories she has gathered throughout the course of her life, including insights God has given her. It's a book filled with spiritual gems.

At one point, she relates the story of a man who was having a conversation about counterfeit money. He was at Scotland Yard, and said to one of the officers there, "It must take years of studying counterfeits before you can quickly recognize the real thing." The response was, "No, quite the contrary. It takes years of studying the real thing to make sure one can spot a counterfeit." That is what we need to do: study the real thing. We need to know the truth, because the best response to a lie is the truth.

Live by the Truth Every Day

Another facet of "girding up the belt of truth," as we put on our spiritual armor, is to live the truth. In other words, live truthfully before God. Put on the belt of truthfulness! Be truthful with God and truthful with other people.

It is absolutely essential for us to be honest with God. We can never pull the wool over God's eyes. We can never fool Him, and never deceive Him. It's as futile as Adam hiding in the garden, acting as if the Lord did not know where he was. It's so foolish when we hide behind our excuses, or busyness, or anything else. God sees everything; He knows everything. The only way to approach God is truthfully. Be honest with the Lord. Be truthful with Him.

Never forget that Jesus saved His most scathing words for the religious hypocrites of the day, the Pharisees. He called their bluff. Essentially He said, "Look boys, I know what's really going on with you. You're white-washed sepulchers, you look good on the outside but inside you are dead. You are decomposing."

It is interesting that the word, "hypocrite" which comes to us from the Greek language, means "an actor" or "one with two faces." You might come to church wearing your Christian face, impressing all your friends with your worship, your spiritual clichés, and the way you mark your Bible. Meanwhile, you have another face in your home, or out there in the world. You are a hypocrite if you live that way. You are lying to God and you are lying to yourself. God sees right through it.

THE BREASTPLATE OF RIGHTEOUSNESS

So be truthful! Be honest! Gird up your life with truth, and tighten your belt, because as we engage in the invisible war, we have another piece of invisible armor to attach to it. It is the breastplate of righteousness. The enemy's tactic of lies is affectively counteracted by the belt of truth. The breastplate of righteousness repels his tactic of accusation. It is interdependent with the belt. I must be truthful with the Lord, avoiding sham, hypocrisy and gameplaying, in order to put this breastplate on.

It's Given Because We're Vulnerable

The breastplate is very important. As Roman armor, it protected the vital organs of the soldier. It guarded his heart and lungs, among other things. If the breastplate wasn't on properly, one well-placed blow could put you down and it would all be over, then and there. Likewise, Satan can take us out in one blow, if we don't keep on this breastplate.

89

How could he do that? Suppose Satan comes to you and says, "You know, you're not worthy to approach God. You've sinned, you failed, you don't measure up. God won't hear your prayers." You know he's right, in a sense. It's true that we've sinned but he's dead wrong about our worthiness before God. Let me make one thing perfectly clear: Every Christian will continue sinning to the bitter end. The Bible does not teach sinless perfection, but that fact does not constitute a license for choosing to sin.

I John tells us, "If we continually, habitually, willfully sin, we are of the devil and we don't know God."

The Bible warns against ongoing sin in Romans 6:

Shall we continue to sin, that God's grace may abound [overflow]? God forbid! How shall we who are dead to sin live any longer in it?

God has not given us a license to sin. God has provided His Holy Spirit to enable us to live differently. Even so, He makes an allowance for us when we sin because, even though we try to live righteously and please the Lord, we still fail. Though we may avoid the more blatant sins of lying and deception, stealing and killing, we still may fall prey to the more subtle sins of self-righteousness and pride. Therefore, God makes a provision which is given to us in I John 2:1,

> If any man sins, we have an Advocate with the Father, Jesus Christ the righteous, and He is the propitiation [the atoning sacrifice] for our sins.

John is saying, "Brothers, we are writing these things to you that you may not sin, but if any man sins, we have an Advocate." It is not a contradiction; he is saying, "I am writing this to you so you don't habitually, continually, willfully sin, but when you stumble and fall by accident, you have an Advocate."

It's Given Because of Jesus

Let's go back to the breastplate. What is it for? The devil fires a flaming arrow at you by saying, "You don't deserve to go to God. You are a failure. You haven't done all that you should do. God won't hear you, you miserable sinner." But his arrow of accusation is repelled by the breastplate of righteousness. I think Paul explains it clearly in Philippians 3:9 where he says,

> I have been found in Him, not having my own righteousness, which is of the law, but that which is through the faith of Jesus Christ, the righteousness which is of God by faith.

I don't respond to the devil by saying, "Now listen here, I read my Bible today and I prayed, so I'm fine." No. My righteousness and worthiness before God has nothing to do with what I have done for God. It has everything to do with what God has done for me.

> Yes, I am sinful.
> Yes, I am unworthy.
> Yes, I am undeserving.

But, God has made provision for my sin. Romans 8:1 states, "There is therefore now no condemnation to those who are in Christ Jesus."

As far as our approach to God is concerned, we acknowledge that we don't deserve acceptance, but we also remember Hebrews 10:19,

> Having boldness to enter into the Holy of Holies, by the blood of Jesus, by a new and living way which He has made for us through the veil, let us draw near, with a true heart and full assurance of faith, having our hearts cleansed from an evil conscience.

We approach Christ on the basis of the blood of Jesus, not on the basis of our own personal righteousness. We don't deserve His love and forgiveness. Like the prodigal, we say, "I am no longer worthy to be called Your son," but God's response is to embrace us, to forgive us and to smother us with kisses. He simply says, "You are My child."

FOOTWEAR FOR THE FIGHT

We have the belt tightened. We have the breastplate attached. Now, we need some footwear. In Ephesians 6:15, Paul instructs, "Have your feet shod with the preparation of the gospel of peace."

There are many kinds of footwear, each one designed for a specific purpose. The footwear Paul describes for us is essential to our survival.

Shoes Give Stability

The sandals of a Roman soldier were simply constructed. It was just a leather sole strapped to his leg by strands of leather, but on the bottom of the sole were studs or nails. The purpose of the studs were to provide the soldier with a firm foundation that would prevent him from slipping or sliding. If he was moving up an incline, he could dig his studded sandals in and hold his ground. This would prove particularly important if he should meet his enemy.

Shoes Give Protection

These Roman sandals served another purpose as well. They not only gave firm footing, but they furnished protection. Sometimes in a battle, the enemy would sharpen sticks and implant them in the ground, sticking up at an angle. If you were to be marching across a field and step on one of those, it caused excruciating pain, to say the least. These were "first century land mines." If you wounded your foot, you would be seriously immobilized. Worse yet, if the injury were severe enough, infection could set in, or loss of blood could cost you your life.

The Gospel Gives Spiritual Stability

Sandals, as common and routine as they may seem, were none-the-less crucial for the affective soldier. In the same way, we must strap on our spiritual sandals. They give us stability and firm-footedness.

92

Notice again that Paul said in Ephesians 6:14, "Stand, therefore." First of all, we need to learn to stand, but there will be temptations to go in the wrong direction. For example, old friends may try to pull us back into a previous lifestyle. "Come on, just go out with us one time. Just have one beer. It'll be fun." Do this. Think that. Read this. Watch that. Giving in, even a little, can be the beginning of a downhill fall. It is interesting that the Bible calls this kind of behavior "backsliding." It's not like jumping off a cliff as much as it is beginning to slip, then gaining momentum as you go. It accelerates day after day. We have to hold our ground because if we don't, the next thing we know, we're sliding, and we can't stop ourselves.

The Christian life is an uphill battle. Either we are climbing or we are slipping. If you try to put yourself into neutral, you're going to go downhill all too quickly! It will amaze you how quickly you can reach the bottom of the pit if you don't continue to climb and grow and mature in your relationship with God.

The Gospel Gives Spiritual Mobility

Our spiritual sandals not only provide stability, they also provide mobility—the ability to move forward at a moment's notice. We need mobility to share the gospel with others and to minister to those in need. We are soldiers in God's army, and we are not only supposed to hold our ground, we are under orders to gain ground. I Peter 3:15 says, "Always be ready to give a defense, to everyone who asks you a reason for the hope that is in you."

Always be ready. Be on guard. Be on duty at all times.

Romans 10:14 says,

How shall they call on Him in whom they have not believed? How shall they believe in Him of whom they have not heard? How shall they hear without a preacher? How shall they preach unless they be sent? As it is written: "How beautiful are the feet of those who preach the gospel of peace, who bring glad tidings of good things!"

The Gospel Gives Protection

Feet enable us to stand. Feet carry us forward. We are called to move forward spiritually. We are to advance the truth. We are to share with others what God has given to us. We are to be ready to give to every man an answer. Some of us may have on our belt but not our breastplate; we may have on our belt and breastplate but we aren't wearing our sandals. It's time to tie them on and begin to move forward.

PUT YOUR ARMOR ON

The shoes God gives are "the preparation of the gospel of peace." It is very important to take note of this: If we are in doubt about our own personal salvation, we'll never be able to fight the enemy. We'll spend all that time struggling with self. A lot of us are fighting on two fronts.

In World War II, Nazi Germany made the critical mistake of getting into war on two fronts at the same time and they lost miserably. Some of us are in a similar war. We are fighting with God and we are fighting with the devil. On one hand, you may be fighting Satan, trying to stay away from things that are sinful, but on the other hand, you are fighting God; you are not surrendering to Him. You are not turning everything over to Him.

This is an impossible situation. You don't know which way to go. It's impossible to have peace. Instead, you are agitated, frustrated and full of anxiety. Once you've surrendered to God, you

93

will have the resources and the power you need to go into battle against the enemy with:

 the belt of truth protecting you from the enemy's lies;

the breastplate of righteousness guarding you from his accusations;

 the sandals of the gospel firmly planting you in the peace of God and enabling you to communicate God's message to the world.

Suit up! Time is of the essence.

CHAPTER

7

*Armed With Faith
And Salvation*

We've looked closely at three of the six pieces of invisible armor which Paul describes in Ephesians six. They are for our protection in the invisible war and we've seen how the belt, the breastplate and the sandals equip us for battle.

The first century soldier always kept his sandals, his belt and his breastplate on. He never took them off. The other three pieces of armor—the shield of faith, the helmet of salvation, and the sword of the Spirit—were to be taken up when needed. You will notice that distinction made in verse 16, "Above all, taking the shield of faith...."

THE SHIELD OF FAITH

Paul makes a transition here saying, "The piece of armor I'm pointing out to you now is different." When we get serious about God, and serious about the spiritual realm, we enter into a new arena. We become a far more formidable foe against the enemy than we ever were before. The devil says, "You want to play hardball? I have a few more tricks up my sleeve. Let's see how long you can stand on the battlefield."

In the face of this threat, we come to Ephesians 6, verse 16:

Above all, take up the shield of faith with which you will be able to quench all the fiery darts of the wicked one.

Temptation Threatens Our Spirits

"Above all" means that you are now in a new arena. The battle is going to heat up and you'd better be prepared. Take up this shield; you're going to need it! The Roman soldier's shield was made of wood. They were large rectangular objects, about four feet high and two feet wide. They were extremely heavy because the wood had a protective metal coating on the outside to repel flaming arrows that might lodge in it. The metal served as fireproofing and protected the soldier from the arrows of the enemy.

Roman soldiers often linked their shields together, and behind them, archers fired their arrows through the openings. This created a sort of moving wall, firing out arrows. Paul's reference to fiery darts relates to one of the most commonly used enemy tactics of his day. Prior to an actual face-to-face engagement with the enemy, sword–to–sword and hand–to–hand, a warrior would often encounter a barrage of flaming arrows coming from all directions. Their sole purpose was to demoralize and confuse him. The Roman soldier had to hold up his shield to protect himself from those arrows. This preliminary attack always occurred before the enemy confronted his combatant directly.

God did not give us breastplates to repel fiery arrows because the breastplate was made of leather and a flaming arrow embedded in a leather breastplate could obviously do great damage. However, by raising the shield with its protective coating, the arrows could be stopped. In spiritual terms, Satan is going to fire his flaming arrows at us. A more contemporary translation would be, "his guided missiles." He is going to set his cross hairs on you and open fire. The specific piece of armor that God has given to deal with these arrows is the shield of faith. We all watched with amazement the accuracy of the missiles and bombs which landed on Baghdad in 1991 during "Operation Desert Shield," fought in the persian Gulf. Some missiles had small television cameras in them, guiding them to their intended targets. We heard of "smart bombs" with pinpoint accuracy, going down airshafts in buildings. Be forewarned! Satan also is very accurate with his "flaming missiles of sin"!

What symbolic things could these arrows represent? They could be arrows of immorality, hatred, envy, pride, covetousness, doubt, worry or any other kind of sin. They come in all sizes and shapes but often they come in the realm of thoughts. You can wake up in the morning and the enemy can hit you with a fiery dart before your feet hit the floor. It might be an impure thought; it might be a thought of hatred toward someone; it might be a blasphemous thought. You're shocked! "How could I think of something like that so early in the morning?" You feel a little guilty about it.

Then of course, the devil, the accuser of the brethren, says, "How could you think of something like that so early in the morning? What's wrong with you? What kind of a Christian are you, anyway?" Now that is very clever. First, he fires the arrow, and then he condemns us for being hit with it!

It is not a sin to be tempted. Even Jesus was tempted, and He was without sin. Those temptations are fiery darts and flaming arrows.

FAITH HAS THE ANSWER

Bible Reading Builds Strength

The devil will also assault you at strategic times. He'll hit you with a barrage of arrows when he doesn't want you to do something, such as reading the Bible. Isn't it amazing that you can open the newspaper and maintain your full ability to concentrate with no distractions? You can get through the whole thing, even the want ads, the comics, all the advertisements they put in it—everything! You may watch some mindless television program and you'll get through it with no phone calls, no distractions, no problems.

Yet, the moment you pull out the Bible, the arrows start flying. It might be inability to concentrate. It might be a hundred and one things you should be doing that come to mind. They aren't necessarily evil thoughts, just, "Oh boy! I forgot to go do this; I've got to pick up the cleaning; I've got to... etc., etc." All these thoughts are arrows, and they are nothing less than an onslaught to get you away from the Word. It was written in someone's Bible, "Sin will keep you from this Book or this Book will keep you from sin." Satan wants to keep you from the Book.

If we likened it to a battle, it would be as if the enemy tried to take your sword away from you. He might want to rob you of your desire to use it, or take away the familiar feel of using it. He might get you to neglect it until it rusted or lost its edge.

Church Attendance Adds Unity

Another way the enemy's arrows fly is by keeping us out of fellowship with God's people. Just try to go to church! It is amazing how many complications can develop.

You go to the movies; no problem.

You go to church; everything goes wrong.

You can't find your keys;

you misplace your wallet or your Bible;

the kids are upset;

you have an argument with your spouse;

you feel like a hypocrite

The arrows are flying! Understand that. Brace yourself for it and determine that you are going to accomplish what you've started. The enemy wants to keep you from fellowship and worship with God's people.

Prayer Builds Spiritual Muscle

The enemy also wants to keep you from prayer. Don't the arrows fly when you try to pray? We need to realize that as we begin to pray and brace ourselves with our shields of faith. When I'm "hit by arrows" (so to speak), I feel that it's a sign that I'm on the right track. When these guided missles from hell hit, we don't want them to hit our breastplate, but our shield, because it was specifically designed to repel them.

The shield is called "faith." I Peter 5:8 says,

> Be sober, be vigilant; because your adversary, the
> devil, walks about like a roaring lion, seeking whom
> he may devour. Resist him, steadfast in the faith....

Then we are told in I John 5:4, "This is the victory that overcomes the world —our faith."

Often, we rely too heavily on our feelings. We stand on our emotions. We stand on our circumstances and we fail, but "faith is the substance of things hoped for, the evidence of things not seen."

Faith looks beyond circumstances.
Faith looks beyond our ups and downs.
Faith looks beyond feelings.
Faith looks at what God can do.

Faith is believing that God not only CAN do it, but that God WILL do it!

MEN WHO HAD A SHIELD OF FAITH

JOSHUA

Consider the story of Joshua when God gave His people the battleplan for taking Jericho, their first conquest. Imagine you were in Joshua's shoes. As he looked at the circumstances of Jericho, he must have felt overwhelmed.

"How are we going to bring down this walled city, Lord? It's too much! What is your battleplan? Attack it? How about if some guys come up from the front, and some others from the back, and they all climb the walls at once? Is that the idea?"

"MARCH AROUND IT AND BLOW TRUMPETS!" God tells Joshua.

Now that took faith, but it was God's strategy. So, they marched around day after day, no doubt being mocked by the people of Jericho. Nevertheless, their faith saw beyond the seeming foolishness and believed God—simply because God said to do it. Faith takes God at His Word.

100 NOAH

Think about Noah building the Ark. Did you know that when Noah began building the Ark, there had never been any rain? Yet, here he was building an ark out in the middle of the desert sands. Like Joshua, Noah faced mockery day after day, but faith looked beyond the circumstances to what God had said. By faith, Noah believed God.

ABRAHAM

Think of Abraham, pushing 100 years old, waiting for the child that God had promised to be born. One day Abraham said, "Lord you aren't doing too well. I'll help you out." He gave God a little assistance by taking Hagar, his wife's maid, to himself. She conceived a child and named him Ishmael.

Consider the problems we continue to see between the descendents of Ishmael and Isaac. They are still at each others' throats! You see, that is not what God told Abraham to do. He told him to wait because from him would come One whose descendants would be innumerable,

■ more than the sand of the sea,

■ more than the stars in the sky.

We Must Have the Shield of Faith

Faith learns to trust in God,

to wait on God,
to look beyond problems,
to see past circumstances,
to rise above emotions.

Faith is what we use to repel enemy attacks; it is the shield. Faith enables us to quickly apply what we believe in order to repel anything the devil does or attempts to do to us.

WHAT WE DON'T NEED

We Don't Need Faith in the Shield

I'm not talking about having "faith in faith." There are some people who tell us that the answer to all our problems is faith. No matter what problems you are encountering, they will exhort you, "It's a lack of faith. You don't have the finances you need? It's a lack of faith. You're not healed? It's a lack of faith. Brother, you need faith!"

Some misguided teachers speak of faith as an absolute panacea, a cure all. They tell us, "Faith is the answer to everything!" They act as if faith were some mystical power we are able to harness, causing the Creator of the Universe to be subservient to our desires and plans.

"Just claim it by faith, and believe it, and God is bound to do it," they boldly assert. That is not what the Bible teaches! Faith is a tool I use to connect myself to God.

The idea here is not to put faith in faith, but to have faith in God. I am to hold up that shield and to take God at His Word.

We Don't Need Doubts About God

Let's reflect back on the Garden of Eden again for a moment, thinking about Satan's temptation of Adam and Eve. He was seeking to undermine their faith. He was trying to get them to doubt God and to trust his lies instead. He was asking them to question God which is the opposite of having faith.

Many of our temptations have their foundation in this one. Begin to doubt or to mistrust God, and you're likely to turn your back on Him and return to the enemy's clutches.

Satan even sought to do this to Jesus in the wilderness. He tried to get Him:

 to doubt God's provision;

to doubt God's protection;

to doubt God's plan;

to doubt God in general.

Faith and doubt don't make good bedfellows. They cannot and will not coexist. If faith comes in the front door, doubt goes out the back. Conversely, if you want to allow doubt to be a part of your **102** life, then you will have to push out faith. The two cannot remain side–by–side. One cancels out the other automatically.

Focus on Jesus

Many years ago on the Sea of Galilee, Peter was walking on the water. He was literally walking by faith. When he sank in the water, he was in doubt. His faith was reactivated once he looked to Jesus Christ. Faith is restored the moment we focus on Him; the minute we look at His Word and remember what He has said to us.

Focus on His Word

For example, if we need His provision, we don't just look at our circumstances. We believe His Word, because there we read His promise in Philippians 4:19: "He will provide for our needs according to His riches in glory through Jesus Christ."

If we are doubtful of our safety and protection, we should come back to Psalm 91. This particular Psalm offers words of comfort and the promise of God's protection to every one of His children. When Satan says to us, "You are going to fail; you are going to fall; you are going to be a casualty; you are not going to make it as a Christian," we can come back to God's promise that "He which has begun a work in you will complete it..." and that "He is the Author and the Finisher of our faith."

In essence, we are saying to Satan, "No, I don't believe you, enemy! I won't listen to your lies. I am putting my faith in God and in His Word."

THE HELMET OF SALVATION

As we hold up the shield of faith, it repels the devil's flaming arrows. The barrage of flaming arrows usually strikes before the actual confrontation with the enemy and that brings us to our next piece of armor, the helmet of salvation. Once the arrows have hit, you can count on the fact that the enemy is on the move. You'd better put on your helmet and you'd better do it quickly because you are about to be engaged in full combat.

This helmet of biblical times was a cap made of leather, embedded with pieces of metal. It was designed to withstand a crushing blow to the head. Many times in battle, the enemy would try to crush the skull, or if possible, to decapitate the person.

103

Helmets Provide Protection

There is a lot of controversy today about wearing helmets when riding a motorcycle. A lot of people don't want to wear them. They like the feel of the wind blowing through their hair. I guess they also like the feel of their head hitting a concrete post at sixty miles an hour. What "matchless exhilaration" it must be to fly off your motorcycle without a helmet and hit something head first! I think I'll pass.

I used to ride dirt bikes, and I earned the nickname, "Crash Laurie." You can imagine how I got that name. While I was out riding full throttle across the desert, it wasn't unusual for the bike to go one way and for me to go another. Sometimes, I was fully airborne. I kept hitting trees and rocks with my head but, fortunately, I had my helmet on. I wasn't really injured, I just got a throbbing headache. Eventually, I evaluated how much fun I was really having.

Salvation Provides Protection

If you ride a motorcycle, a helmet can save your life. A helmet can also save your life in the heat of spiritual battle. It seems clear that when Paul speaks of a helmet he is referring to protection of the brain, the mind, the thinking and the understanding of the

Christian. That's because Satan recognizes the value of getting a foothold in the realm of the thoughts and the imagination.

He knows this will prepare the way for thoughts to be translated into actions. He knows if he can get you to think about it, he is a step closer to getting you to do it. It says in Proverbs 23:7, "As a man thinks in his heart, so is he."

Protection For The Heart

Jesus really pulled the mask off the Pharisees in this regard. They would sit around and congratulate themselves because they'd never committed adultery or murdered anyone. They never engaged in adulterous acts and they never murdered, yet their hearts were filled with lustful thoughts and with hatred. Jesus really blew their cover when he said, "You have heard that it has been said, 'Thou shall not commit adultery.' Well, I say unto you, If you look on a woman with lust in your heart, you have already committed adultery."

That hurts! He's saying that as far as God is concerned, if you are thinking about it, you are already sinning. If you think about sin, fantasize about sin, lust over someone or something, the question I would ask you is, "Why don't you just go ahead and do it?" Many times it's only because we don't want to get caught. We're afraid of the repercussions.

I heard on the radio once that for some, the percentage of sexual activity outside marriage among Americans is decreasing because of the fear of AIDS. They've tried every kind of so-called "safe sex" they can think of, sought out every way of staying immoral and not pay the price, but many people realize it is like playing Russian roulette with a bullet in every chamber. I'm glad the promiscuity rate is going down. However, the real problem is that people would still do those things, if they didn't have to pay the price.

Protection For The Mind

The point is, sin is more than just actions and deeds. It's something within the heart and mind that leads to action. And there's a good reason that the mind and the thoughts need to be protected because, if the threat of repercussions is removed, you will commit that sin! God wants to go deeper. He doesn't just want to stop your actions. He wants to change your heart so you're no longer desiring and thinking about those things.

The way He does that is by providing us with the helmet of salvation. When I wear my helmet as a soldier in the invisible war, I will not entertain thoughts that are sinful or spiritually harmful. Although it is true that I can't stop an impure or sinful thought from knocking on the door of my imagination, I can surely stop it from moving in and making a home there! I can't stop temptation, but I can refuse to dwell on it.

That's where the helmet of salvation comes in. II Corinthians 10:4 says,

> For the weapons of our warfare are not physical but mighty in God for pulling down strongholds, so cast down imaginations and every high thing that sets itself against the knowledge of God, and lead captive every thought to the obedience of Christ.

We are to repel those things that would be spiritually destructive by bringing every thought captive to the obedience of Jesus Christ. Watch what you think about! Too many people are emptyheaded, allowing any thought or influence to enter their minds. They may think that it doesn't really affect them but, of course, it does. The Bible says, "You will reap what you sow...and if you sow to the flesh you will reap corruption," literally "rottenness." To be carnally minded is "death," the Bible says, and you will be affected.

Spiritually speaking, what have you been thinking about? What are you filling your mind with?" You might say, "I can't understand why I am always having impure, lustful thoughts or hateful, greedy thoughts." What are you listening to? Let's go through some of your cassettes or CD's. What content is there? You might say,"Well, I just like the music, the beat, you know. The words don't affect me." Sure they do! They lodge in your self-conscious more than you will ever know.

Protection For The Eyes

With regard to things that we observe and absorb, we have to be selective; we have to be careful. You might want to invest in some good Christian praise and worship music to play in your car. When you are driving down the road, singing and praising the Lord, it can even make a traffic jam tolerable. The Bible is available on cassette. You can put it in your player and listen to the Word of God. Now when you hear the Scripture, when you hear music that glorifies God, don't you know that's going to build you up? Philipians 4:8 says,

106

> Finally brothers, whatsoever things are true, noble, just, pure and lovely, and good report if there is any virtue in them, anything praiseworthy, think on these things.

Isaiah 26:3 tells us,

> Be anxious for nothing but in prayer and supplication, with thanksgiving, let your requests be made known to God and the peace of God, which surpasses all understanding, will keep your hearts and minds in Christ Jesus.

Protection From The World

Are you tempted to worry? Worry is rooted in doubting God. Instead of allowing worry to fill your mind, take that same energy and apply it to prayer. Commit that need or concern to God in prayer and the peace of God will keep your heart and mind through Christ Jesus.

Protection From Condemnation

The helmet is called *salvation*. Salvation is in the past present and future. God has saved me from sin, from my past and from myself. My Heavenly Father is saving me on a daily basis, which means that He is delivering me from potential disaster by keeping me in His care. He is protecting His investment, by changing me into His image.

He will also save me in the future from the wrath to come. Salvation is not only something He has done for me, it is something He is *doing* for me, and it is something He will *yet do* for me in the future. Salvation is a continual process.

Put the hope of salvation in your life! Buckle on that helmet and live in the safety of what God is accomplishing.

107

CHAPTER

Taking The Offensive

f it were possible for you to look at yourself in a spiritual mirror and if you've donned the armor we've described, you'd find yourself almost completely outfitted for battle. The only thing lacking is "the sword of the Spirit."

This important piece of equipment is not only a defensive weapon used to deflect the blows of the enemy, but it is also an offensive one. It should be noted that this is the only offensive weapon we are given. If the enemy is coming, you don't want to throw your helmet at him; your head would be unprotected. You wouldn't attempt to take him out with your shield or beat him with your sandal. However, God has given us a weapon for the fight; it is called " the sword of the Spirit."

110

A SWORD FOR THE BATTLE

Many believers have all their armor in place but they never use their sword. They leave it in the sheath. They talk about it, study it or compare swords with each other, but they never actually utilize the sword in spiritual battle. As I have already stated, we must learn to be more than just defenders; we need to be aggressors. The person who is in a defensive position, is at a disadvantage in battle. He is simply waiting for the enemy's next attack, hoping he'll survive. The aggressor has the advantage of taking the initiative. He can choose the time and place of the attack which places him in a superior position.

In every battle, there is a decisive moment when it turns into a victory or a defeat. Too many of us are only trying to hold ground, only trying to defend ourselves, always in a defensive mode. We need to learn how to attack; how to move forward. As we get our orders from our commander and chief, we can seize the moment.

God's Word is Effective

Keep this in mind: Whether we know the value of our sword or not, Satan does. He will do everything he can to see that either we keep our swords sheathed or that we don't put them on in the first place. Satan frequently directs his attacks toward the Word of God in the lives of believers, because he knows its effectiveness in battle. He will seek to interrupt your study of the Word. He will try to keep you from memorization of it. He will try to stop you from meditating on Scripture. He knows the powerful effect these activities can have.

He has read II Timothy 3:16: "All Scripture is God-breathed, and is powerful." He also realizes that Isaiah 55:11 is true. God says,

> "My Word shall not return void, but it will prosper in the place that I send it and accomplish what I please."

Your adversary does not want you to learn to use this mighty weapon. Satan is well aware that God's Word is:

> Sharper than any two-edged sword, piercing even to the division of soul and spirit, and of the joints and the marrow, and it is a discerner of the thoughts and the intent of the heart.

In the parable of the sower (Matthew 13), Jesus told about seed that fell on different kinds of ground. Some seed came to rest on the hard, beaten ground of the path, and the birds came and picked it up and ate it. It never took root. Jesus said, "These are the people that hear the Word of God, but Satan is quick to snatch it from them."

How he tries to do that with us!

He tries to snatch it away;
>   to prevent us from grasping it;
>   to keep us from understanding it.

Later on in the same parable, Jesus talked about seed that was cast on stony ground. It shot up quickly but because of the rock, it was barely able to penetrate the soil. It had insufficient roots to survive. He said,

> "These are they that hear the Word of God and immediately receive it with joy but, when affliction or persecution comes because of the Word, immediately they fall away."

God's Word Is Accurate

It comes back to the Word. Satan wants to keep you from really appropriating it in your life. That is why he challenged the Word of God in the Garden of Eden, saying to Eve, "Hath God said?" And that is why certain liberal theologians are doing the devil's bidding when they change the wording of Scripture to fit their warped concepts of what it should be saying. A group of these "scholars" recently got together and decided that Jesus never said that He was coming back again. This, of course, would have been quite surprising to Jesus. Nevertheless, that is what they decided. These misguided men remove from Scripture whatever does not please them. They are tampering with God's Word and undermining the trust that people have in Scripture. As a result, intentionally or unintentionally, they are doing the work of the enemy himself.

112

The Scripture warns us against such a thing in Proverbs 30, which says, "Every word of God is tested. Do not add to His words, lest He reprove you and you be found a liar."

God's Word Is Alive

The Sword of the Spirit is not just the Word, it is the Word activated and interpreted by the Holy Spirit. This is an important point. Only the Holy Spirit can give us the understanding of the Scriptures, enabling us to use the Word of the Sword properly. You could be a good scholar or even a genius, and yet be unable to understand the words of Scripture. The Bible says,

> The natural man perceives not the things of God, neither can he know them because they are spiritually discerned.

This can be frustrating because there are times when we try to communicate our faith to non-believers and they just can't comprehend what we are saying; they cannot grasp it. This happens because they are not spiritually awakened.

By contrast, the Bible says (I Corinthians 2:9-10),

"Eye hath not seen nor has ear heard, neither has it entered into the heart of man the things that God has prepared for them that love Him, but God has revealed them unto us by His Spirit, for the Spirit searches all things, yes, the deep things of God."

God can reveal things to you from Scripture that a person who is not a believer could never see. Even a theologian will never get hold of it unless his spiritual eyes are open. A child sometimes has a better spiritual understanding than an educated person. I think of people who have not had the advantage of advanced education in third world countries, who have simply taken the Word of God at face value and are seeing miracles. They see God's Word confirmed, and observe mighty things transpiring.

How unfortunate that they have not been able to come and attend some of our liberal seminaries! Some non-believing professor could tear the Word apart for them so they'd realize that it really doesn't mean what it says. Poor "ignorant" people, actually taking God at His word! Maybe they could teach us a few things!

God's Word and the Spirit Agree

It is important for us to find a balance between the Spirit and the Word. Two camps seem to have developed within the Church. One group puts all its emphasis on the Spirit. The other puts all its emphasis on the Word. Those who put so much emphasis on the Spirit that they neglect the Word often have "Holy Spirit seminars." They talk about the Spirit and sing about the Spirit, and their estimation of a good church service is represented by how many utterances in tongues or prophecies there were. How long did the worship go on? Were there any miracles? Any signs? Any wonders? Did they "feel" His presence? The problem is that often these are things that are being orchestrated by man, and not directed by God's Spirit.

Don't get me wrong. I believe in the Holy Spirit and I believe the gifts of the Spirit are for today. I believe in miracles; I have seen them many times and I know God is able to do them. That's just the point: God can do it; I don't have to do for Him.

I don't have to put on "pretend" miracles or try to psyche people up to a fever pitch. I prefer to allow God's Spirit to do the miracles. As a pastor and evangelist, He's simply called me to teach and to preach the Word, but there are those who will attempt to orchestrate these things.

We Must Recognize The Spirit

I've seen newspaper ads for churches which say something like: "REVIVAL THIS WEEK." I find this curious because I believe "revival" is something that God does sovereignly. However, these churches have figured out how to put on a "revival"! Their ads sometimes read, "REVIVAL MONDAY THROUGH FRIDAY, STARTS AT 7:00 ENDS AT 9:00!!" "MIRACLES WILL TAKE PLACE: THE BLIND WILL SEE, THE DEAF WILL HEAR, THE DEAD WILL BE RAISED." I'm sorry, but I have a problem with that.

Don't accuse me of doubting the work of God. I don't. However, I do have my doubts about the work of man. Many times people get themselves so emotionally involved that they just take over. The Holy Spirit has little to do with that kind of experience. It would be unwise to make a blanket condemnation of all such services; each one is individual. Nevertheless, it is necessary to discern between the work of the flesh and the work of the Spirit.

It is interesting that in the book of Acts, we never read of a miracle that was announced ahead of time. For example, when John and Peter went to the Beautiful Gate and through them, Jesus healed the crippled man; they were just going about their own business. We aren't told that Peter said, "Now listen, John, go down to the Jerusalem Post, take out a full page ad. Here's my photo. Put that in and say that we're going to heal this man. He's going to leap and walk and he's going to praise God. Let's get the word out! Let's tell them a miracle is coming!" That isn't what they did.

The miracle came as God directed them in their daily activity. In the book of Acts, the Church never focused on miracles. They focused on Christ and on teaching His Word. They let God do the miracles, in His way and in His time.

Believers should not follow signs and wonders. Signs and wonders should follow believers.

We Must Know The Word of God

If a person only focuses on the Holy Spirit, without the balance of the Word, he becomes susceptible to false teaching. He lacks a good foundation in what God has said, and he can become unstable. On the other side of the spectrum, and equally as wrong, are those that look to the Word but don't allow the Spirit to do His work. I've been in churches where doctrinally, the teachings are right on. These are orthodox believers. They believe the right things yet their churches are dead as dead could be. There is no life or vibrancy in the worship service. You would think it was a morticians' convention or a collection of "frozen people" instead of "chosen people." Still, they believe in the Word and they believe the right doctrine. What's wrong? Often, it's because the door is closed to the working of the Spirit.

They might say, "Oh this is the way we've always done things." If someone has a fresh, new worship chorus to introduce, they say, "We can't allow a song like that. We only sing the great hymns of the church. This is the tradition. This is the way we have always done it." The result is that the door is shut on the work of God's Spirit.

One extreme is as wrong as the other. We need both the Word and the Spirit. I've heard it put in a rather simplistic but insightful way:

"Too much Word and you dry up;
   too much Spirit and you blow up;
      enough of both and you grow up."

We need a foundation in the Word but we also need the Holy Spirit to bring it to life. That's why this weapon is called the "Sword of the Spirit." It is God's Word, used aggressively and effectively as we are directed by God's Spirit.

God's Word is Alive

God's Spirit will also help us to bring the Word to life for others. God's Spirit will direct us in what we say as we share the

Word. Jesus promised that the Spirit would bring all things to memory, whatever He has spoken to us. The Holy Spirit brings the appropriate Scripture to mind at the appropriate time. Proverbs 25:11 puts it this way, "A word that is fitly spoken is like apples of gold in settings of silver."

That's very poetic and it tells us how important the Word is when it is shared appropriately. To prepare yourself for this, you must commit the Scripture to memory. Think of how many foolish things we have lodged in our minds, things that have been drilled in. Stupid slogans have been repeated again and again by Madison Avenue on behalf of a thousand different products. I can't get rid of some of this senseless information.

How much better it would be to fill my mind with the Word of God, to commit it to memory. The Psalmist says, "Thy Word have I hid in my heart that I might not sin against You." The wise man of Psalm 1 "continues in the Word day and night." That's what we need to do! If we fill our minds with the Word of God, then the Spirit will have something to draw from, to bring to our memory.

Jesus said He would bring to remembrance whatever He had spoken, but if I haven't taken time to learn what He said, how can He bring it to my memory? You might say, "No problem. He'll just put it there supernaturally." We need a little cooperation here! You should read it! It's really lazy to say He'll just put it there. That's like saying, "Hey, I don't have to work. I'll just sit around like the prophet Elijah and wait for some ravens to bring me a Big Mac!" The Bible teaches that if you don't work you shouldn't eat. You are violating a biblical principle and God won't honor it.

The same rule applies to the memorization of Scripture. You should be committing the Word to memory. Then, the Spirit of God will have something in your mind to use during strategic moments in the spiritual battle. You'll have the ammo, so to speak, and you'll know how to use it. Don't find yourself saying, "Well, it says somewhere in the Bible..." or "My pastor once said..." Know the Word of God for yourself!

God's Word is Revealing

In the book of Acts, we have the story of how God used a man named Philip to share His Word. Initially, Philip was directed by God to the desert. He had been having a time of great blessing down in Samaria. The gospel was being preached; miracles were taking place; people were coming to faith. But God said, "Philip, go to the desert." He didn't say "Philip, go to the desert to meet an Ethiopian who went to Jerusalem searching for God but didn't find Him. Instead he found a copy of the Scriptures, and he is going to be reading out loud from Isaiah 53. You'd better brush up on it a little bit because there is a big question he is going to ask you...."

No, God simply said, "Go to the desert." He didn't give Philip a blueprint or tell him what was going to transpire. Such guidance can be difficult because God doesn't always show us His plans for the future. He doesn't tell us everything that will happen. He just leads us just one step at a time.

Philip was obedient. When he got there, the Ethiopian man came by. He was a treasurer for Candace the Queen, and was a man of great influence and power. No doubt he was traveling with a huge entourage on the way. He had come back from Jerusalem. He probably had been seeking God there and hadn't found Him amidst all the dead orthodoxy of the day. The Ethiopian was reading from Isaiah 53, which is one of the Old Testament messianic Scriptures describing the crucifixion of Jesus. He was reading aloud that Jesus would be led as a sheep to slaughter, but he didn't understand the words.

Philip approached him and asked, "Do you understand what you are reading?" The man said, "How can I unless someone helps me and shows me the way? Who was the prophet speaking of? Himself or another?"

Philip might have said, "You know that's a good question, and I don't really have the answer. I'm going to get back to you on that. Give me your FAX number." Fortunately, right there on the spot, Philip pulled out the Sword of the Spirit. He knew Isaiah 53, by committing it to memory and was able to speak decisively and preach Jesus from that Scripture. The Ethiopian man believed God's Word that day.

117

Had Philip not known that Scripture and not known how to use the Sword, the opportunity could have been lost. There are strategic times of opportunity to lead people to Christ, and if we know how to use our Swords, we can seize those opportunities. If we don't, we may have to let them slip by.

You may say, "But, I'm no Bible scholar." That may be true, but it certainly doesn't mean that you shouldn't be a Bible *student*!

God's Word is Essential

The classic example of using the Sword of the Spirit is found in Luke 4, demonstrated by Jesus Himself. He had fasted for forty days and forty nights and the Bible says He was hungry. In actual fact, He was probably at the point of starvation. The devil came to Him and said, "If You are the son of God, turn this rock into a piece of bread." Jesus reached down and pulled the Sword out of the sheath, so to speak. He quoted the Word of God. Appropriately He said, "Man shall not live by bread alone, but by every word that proceeds out of the mouth of God."

118

The devil took Him to a high place and showed Him all the kingdoms of the world and said, "All of this is I will give to You if You will worship me." Jesus, once again setting an example for us, pulled the Sword from the sheath and said, "It is written, thou shall worship the Lord God and Him only shall you serve."

Then, the devil altered his attack somewhat. He began to quote Scripture to Jesus. He took Him to the top of the temple and said,

> "Cast Yourself off from here because it is written [quoting Psalm 91]: `He will give His angels charge over You, to keep You in all Your ways, to bear you up lest You dash Your foot against a stone.'"

That was a clever ploy. It was out of context and it wasn't accurate, but it was Scripture and it seemed relevant. However, Jesus brought the entire issue to an abrupt conclusion saying, "Thou shall not tempt the Lord thy God."

For each separate temptation, Jesus had the appropriate defense from the Word of God. He knew how to use the Sword, when to slice, when to thrust, when to cut, when to chop.

God's Word is Holy

We need to use the Word just that well, too, because Satan will strike us. He'll tell us that God won't hear us. He might even quote Scripture: "If I regard iniquity in my heart the Lord will not hear me."

Satan may say, "You are guilty, so God won't hear you. Boy, are you defeated!" Ah, but wait! Pull the Sword out and open the pages to I John 1:9,

> If we confess our sin, He is faithful and just to forgive us our sin and to cleanse us from all unrighteousness!

Perhaps the devil has told you that you're condemned. You've sinned. You've failed. Pull the Sword from the sheath and read Romans 8:1, "There is therefore now no condemnation to those who are in Christ Jesus,"

Touché! Satan's lost again, because you knew the Word; you've committed it to memory and you are able to defend yourself.

God's Word is Powerful

When you know the Word, you are not only able to defend yourself but you also know how to use it aggressively. The most effective witness you will ever have in sharing your faith is the witness that is saturated with God's Word. Your opinions and your thoughts are really immaterial, but God's Word will not return void.

> My word will...
> your word will... but
> God's Word will never return void.

God's Word will accomplish it's purpose. That's why we must learn it and use it.

One of the reasons for the phenomonal success of Evangelist Billy Graham, is that he constantly quotes Scripture in his sermons.

We've all seen him in a characteristic stance, Bible held high, proclaiming, "The Bible says..." God has obviously honored the faithful proclamation of Scripture in his life and ministry.

PRAYER - THE ULTIMATE WEAPON

There is one last weapon for this invisible war in which we're all engaged. Paul mentions it, and we must mention it here. Ephesians 6, verse 18 says,

> Praying always with all prayer and supplication in
> the Spirit, being watchful to this end with all
> perseverance and supplication for all the saints.

120

This brings us full circle in our study of spiritual warfare. Remember the original concept, "Stand in the Lord and in the power of His might." This same idea is here as we are told to pray.

Prayer brings us back to total trust and dependence on God. Even with all that armor on: sandals tied and belt tightened, breastplate shiny and all the rest of it, we might start feeling a little self-confident. We might be thinking, "No one can bring me down! I'm invincible. I know my Bible. I'm walking with God; I'm living righteously before God. My armor is all in place. Nothing will defeat me,"

Our enemy says, "I like your attitude." This attitude plays right into his hands. The areas where we think we're the strongest are often the areas in which we are the most vulnerable. You might say, "I would never be unfaithful to my spouse. I would never lie. I would never steal. I would never fall for this or that." Just be careful!

When you start boasting about things you would "never" do, think of Simon Peter's boastful claim, "Though all deny You Lord, I, Simon, will never deny You!" You recall, Peter didn't deny the Lord once, not twice, but three times. He even took an oath saying he never knew Him! In the very area where Peter thought he was the strongest, he turned out to be the most defenseless. That is why the Scripture warns us, "Let him that thinks he stands, take heed lest he fall."

Pray in the Spirit. Come back to total trust and reliance upon God. Don't trust in your armor. Your armor is utterly useless unless you depend upon the Lord, Himself. There's an old hymn that says,

"Each piece put on with prayer." A large part of the spiritual battle is fought though prayer. It has been rightly said that the Church marches on its knees. Great spiritual battles can be fought and won in prayer by God's people.

■ Nehemiah recognized this principle when he was surrounded by his enemy. We read that "He made his prayer to God and because of that set a watch against them, day and night."

■ Jehoshaphat, when outnumbered by the enemy, said to the Israelites, "The battle is not yours, but the Lord's." Then he prayed,

"Oh, our God, will You not judge them? We have no might against this great company that comes against us, neither do we know what to do, but our eyes are on You."

121

Trusting in God before a blow is struck, or an arrow is fired, we say, "Lord I'm confident only in You, because I know when I stand in You, I am strong." Look again at Psalm 91:1 which says,

He that dwells in the secret place of the Most High shall abide under the shadow of the Almighty. I will say of the Lord, "He is my refuge and my fortress; my God, in Him will I trust."

As long as I am standing in Him, I have His strength. As soon as I step out from under His protection, I become vulnerable to attack. Jesus pointed this out when He said, "Before you can go in and plunder a man's goods, you have to bind the strong man." In other words, if someone wanted to steal from your home, he would tie you up first. Obviously, you would not want him to take things out of your house, but if he tied you up, you couldn't stop him.

The same principle is true in spiritual warfare. You bind the strong man.

Who is the strong man? The devil.

How do you bind him? Through prayer.

When undertaking any endeavor for Him, we should first pray something like this:

> "Lord, bind the power of Satan and anything that he would seek to do to stop Your Word from going forth and to hinder the work that You want to accomplish."

We do that because we have seen the power of prayer. Pastors, evangelists and missionaries have learned that much of the battle can only be won with the prayers of faithful men and women behind them. As their warriors pray back home, they are free to go out and face the conflict into which God has called them.

122

Satan knows about this power. And he wants to drive a wedge between us and our Commander-in-Chief. He wants to isolate us out in the field. He wants to break down our communications. We must always maintain communication with our Commander–in–Chief, the Lord. He is our source of supply for spiritual food, ammunition, information and orders, and prayer is our means of keeping in close contact with Him.

- Through prayer, we make our needs known.
- Through prayer, we ask help for cooperating forces, for colaborers, for fellow soldiers.
- Through prayer, we confess our defeats.
- Through prayer, we praise Him for victory!

Do you remember when ten lepers were healed, but only one came back to thank Jesus? His question to that one grateful man, was, "Where are the other nine?" I wonder if God still asks that question today. "Where are the other nine? They're always around when they need My help, but after I help them, they don't even come back and thank Me."

Our prayers should praise Him for victories, acknowledging that He is the One who has given it, and our prayers should confess our defeats. When we have failed, we shouldn't make excuses, but we should ask God to forgive us. We need to learn whatever we can from the mistakes we have made. To fail to pray—the sin of prayerlessness—can have serious repercussions.

Joshua and the Children of Israel learned this when they were conned by a group of clever, deceptive people known as the Gibeonites. God had told Israel to defeat all the enemies of the land and drive them out. The Gibeonites quickly realized that they would be destroyed by Israel so they pretended they had come from a far country. They put old tattered shoes on their feet and placed some moldy bread in their bags. They staggered over the top of a hill and said, "We have come from a far country. When we left, this bread was fresh from our ovens. When we left, these shoes were new. Now look at them! We need your help! Won't you make a treaty with us? Enter into a partnership with us!"

Joshua gave them the once-over and thought everything looked all right. The Scripture specifically says, "He failed to consult with the Lord." So he made an agreement, not realizing he was compromising with the enemy. Sometimes things will look perfect and we might say, "The Lord opened all the doors." Maybe so, but the Lord isn't the only one who can open doors. The devil can open them too.

Jonah should also have recognized that. He didn't want to go to Nineveh where God called him. Instead, he went down to Tarshish, running away from God's will. One door after another opened for him, but did God open those doors? No, the enemy opened those doors for Jonah.

Sometimes, the enemy will open doors through circumstances that appear favorable. It might seem like the right thing to do yet it could be a plot, a trap from hell itself. That's why it is so vital that we learn discernment through prayer and study of the Word. Asking God to direct us and to show us His way for us, is not optional. We must pray in the Spirit.

Ephesians 6, verse 18 also says, "Praying always..." We are to live in a continual consciousness of God's presence, enjoying fellowship, communion and friendship with Him.

CONCLUSION

We are to put on our armor, piece by piece, with God's directions in mind as we engage in the invisible war.

- The belt of truth gives freedom of movement. It allows us to live truthfully and honestly before God, and provides us with the truth to give to others.
- The breastplate of righteousness protects our vital organs on the battlefield. We don't stand in our own righteousness, but rather in the righteousness God has given us through Jesus Christ and His work at the cross.
- The sandals He provides give us sure-footedness and stability on the battlefield, and the ability to march forward.
- The shield of faith stops the flaming arrows of the enemy: arrows of doubt, arrows of condemnation, arrows of enticement. We deflect them with our trust and faith in God, not with our emotions and feelings.
- The helmet of salvation protects our minds and our thoughts as we keep them fixed on Him.
- The Sword of the Spirit is our one offensive weapon. Now we can aggressively move in and begin to march!

In the book of Esther, Mordecai said to Queen Esther, "Perhaps it is for such a time as this that you came to the kingdom." Through a miraculous turn of events, Esther found herself in the king's palace at a time when a death sentence had been pronounced upon all of the Jewish people.

This devious scheme came from a man named Haman. Esther, and only Esther, was in a strategic position to turn events around, if she could find the courage to stand up on behalf of her people. She did!

Wherever you work, wherever you live, or whatever people you contact, God has put you in a strategic position "for such a time as this." Every hour of the spiritual battle is strategic. Every day there are moments of decision; chances to witness; occasions to do a work for God. If we are blind to these things, walking around in a dream world, opportunities will pass and we'll never see them.

Let's ask God to give us direction. Let's get our armor on. Let's begin to search out those opportunities. In doing so, we will be moving forward; taking the initiative; striking effectively. We will be soldiers God can use in the invisible, but very real, war we are engaged in.

We will be more than conquerors in Him.

CHAPTER

9

What Happens After Death?

We've been looking behind the veil that separates the visible from the invisible, and the physical from the spiritual. We've considered holy angels and fallen ones. We've explored commonly used tactics and strategies of Satan. We've examined the armor of God, its various pieces, and their value. Now let's reflect upon what happens after life on this earth or simply, what happens after we die?

The word "death" makes a lot of people squirm. Yet death is something every one of us will experience unless Jesus returns and takes those of us, who have trusted Him as our Lord and Savior, to heaven. If He doesn't come back in our generation, we will most certainly die. When we're young, death seems distant and unreal. As time marches on, however, we're reminded that it's getting closer every day.

Have you run into someone you haven't seen for a long time and they say some tactful thing to you like, "You really look older! You have a lot more wrinkles than you did the last time I saw you, and what happened to your hair?" I've heard every "balding" joke ever told, always by people with a full head of hair, of course.

We're also reminded of the aging process when we take out old scrapbooks or home videos. It's true. We look different these days. There are daily physical reminders, too. Teeth begin to decay. Eyesight starts fading. Hair turns grey and begins to recede. So, we get false teeth. We get contact lenses. We dye our hair or wear a hairpiece. The reality is that we are all aging. These frail bodies of ours were not designed to last forever.

In our country, we have an obsession with youth. We want to remain young, or at least look young. We don't even want to grow up, much less get old. Nonetheless, we're getting closer to death with every passing day. C. S. Lewis once pointed out that war does not increase the death toll. Death is total in every generation. Everyone is going to die. George Bernard Shaw wrote, "The statistics on death are quite impressive. One out of every one person dies."

Death seems somewhat unreal in this time of modern technology. You know someone is dead, but when you turn on the television he's still there.

John Wayne is still fighting the bad guys and winning the wars.
Elvis Presley is still singing to us on the radio.
We still hear the voice of John Lennon.
We still see Marilyn Monroe.
We still hear speeches by J.F.K.
We still listen to Martin Luther King, Jr.

It seems like they're still alive, but they're not. They're gone.
Death is a very real thing, and we're all facing it.

We need to think about it. We need to talk about it. Most
importantly, we need to prepare for it.

TWO KINDS OF DEATH

129

The Bible teaches there are actually two deaths. One is
physical death and the other is eternal death. Jesus warned that we are
to fear the second death more than the first one. He described the
second death, hell, as eternal separation from God. He indicated that
the death of our bodies is nothing compared to the conscious,
everlasting banishment of a soul from God.

When you say the word "hell," many people bristle. They
don't like the concept at all. "You believe in that outmoded myth?"
they ask. Some things have been presented to us in such distorted
ways, we tend to dismiss them as fictitious, but the Bible speaks
repeatedly about hell.

It may be controversial;
It may be unpopular,
but it is real.

Did you know that Jesus spoke more about hell than all the
other preachers of the Bible put together? Why? He alone has seen it.
He knows what it's like. He knows the reality of it, and the last thing
He wants is for any of us to spend eternity there.

The Scriptures are filled with references to hell. We read,

"The Son of Man will send forth His angels. They
will gather out of His kingdom all things that offend
and they that do not believe will be cast into a
furnace of fire. There will be wailing and gnashing
of teeth."

The Scriptures say,

"So shall it be at the end of the world, the angels shall come forth and sever the wicked from among the just and shall cast them into a furnace of fire. There will be wailing and gnashing of teeth. They will say of them on the left hand, "Depart from me you who are cursed into everlasting fire prepared for the devil and his angels." In flaming fire God will take vengeance on them that do not know God and obey not the gospel of our Lord Jesus Christ who will be punished with everlasting destruction from the presence of the Lord and from the glory of His power."

Revelation 14:10-11 tells us,

"They will drink of the wine of the wrath of God which is poured out without mixture into the cup of His indignation. And he shall be tormented with fire and brimstone in the presence of the holy angels and in the presence of the Lamb and the smoke of their torment ascends up forever and they have no rest day or night."

We're also told in Revelation 21:8,

"The spirits of the unbelieving, the abominable, murderers, immoral people, sorcerers or those involved with drugs and idolaters and all liars will have their part in the lake that burns with fire and brimstone. This is the second death."

ETERNAL LIFE

Hell is a real place, but it was created for the devil and his angels. God did not create hell for people. He created hell for Satan and all of the fallen angels that have chosen to follow him. God wants you to join Him in heaven. Jesus said,

"In my Father's house are many mansions. If it were not so I would have told you. I go to prepare a place for you. If I go and prepare a place for you, I will come again and receive you unto myself that where I am there you may be also (John 14:2-3)."

In John 17 in His prayer to the Father He said, "Father, my prayer is that they would be with me."

When you're really in love with someone, you want them to share your life with you. When you're married and something great happens, you think, "I can hardly wait to tell my wife." Something good happens; you got a raise; the Lord answered a prayer; you caught the ultimate wave! What do you do? You call your wife or your husband.

131

One day in Southern California, I was out surfing. My wife was on the beach, reading a magazine. I caught the "set wave," which is the largest. I was all alone on that wave, in all my glory. It was one of those slow, rolling waves. I was getting the best wave of my life. My ride was unbelievably long. The wave started to close out, but another wave was inside so I paddled a little bit and caught the second one. Meanwhile, my wife was sitting on the shore, still absorbed in her magazine. I started to yell, as I was surfing this incredible wave, "Cathe, Cathe, look, look!" I really wanted her to see me. As I got closer to the shore, I thought, "This is going to be the greatest wave I've ever ridden and she won't even know!" Coming to the end of my ride, my board came up on the sand and I ran over to my wife exclaiming excitedly, "Cathe, did you see that?"

"See what?" she asked, casually turning the magazine page. My ultimate ride, and she had missed it! I was really disappointed, because I wanted to share it with her.

God loves you and He wants you to share heaven with Him. Jesus said, "My desire is that they would be with me that I might show them my glory." God wants you to be in heaven. The last place He wants you to be is in hell. That is why He took such radical measures to keep us out.

THE SIN PROBLEM

Being a just and holy God, He has a problem with sin. We've all violated His laws, so something had to be done. The Bible teaches, "The soul that sins shall surely die." That is why He sent Jesus to the cross. In essence, God Himself took our place.

It's like being in a court of law. You're standing before the judge, and he's telling you what your sentence is. Then, the judge takes off his robe, puts down his gavel and descends from the bench. As He walks up next to you he says, "I'll go and serve your time." First he brings the judgment, then he comes around and takes it upon himself. That is exactly what happened on the cross of Calvary.

Some people, upon hearing the word "hell" ask, "How could a God of love send a person to hell?" I think Mark Twain spoke for many when he summed it up in this statement,

> "God mouths mercy and yet He invented hell. He speaks about justice and He invented hell. He speaks of golden rules and forgiveness but He invented hell."

Was there inconsistency on the part of God when He invented hell? How could a God of love send us there? It is precisely because He is a God of love and justice that He created hell. He did not create it for people, and if you go there, you have no one to blame but yourself. You're going to have to resist the work of the Holy Spirit throughout your entire life. You're going to have to turn down hundreds, perhaps thousands of opportunities to believe in Him. You're going to have to step over Jesus to get there. If you're bound and determined, you can go to hell. But don't blame God!

Suppose you were very sick and called to make an appointment with your doctor. After waiting in his office, surrounded by sneezing, coughing, sick people and screaming children, your turn finally comes. He diagnoses your problem and prescribes medication. "If you take this medicine, you will recover," he assures you. After the doctor leaves, you think to yourself, "I don't need this medicine. I don't care what he says." You take the prescription and pitch it into the wastebasket. A little more time passes and you get sicker. You see your doctor and he asks you if you took the medicine. You say, "No!

I'm sicker than ever and it's all your fault." The doctor won't agree with you. He told you what to do; he gave you a remedy; you cannot hold him responsible when you refused his remedy. It's your own responsibility.

The Great Physician, Jesus Christ, has given us His remedy for our spiritual illness. It is to repent of our sin and follow Him; to trust in Him; to believe in Him; and to walk with Him. If someone refuses and then ends up in hell, it's his own fault. The Bible says, "How can we escape if we neglect so great a salvation?"

HELL IS AN AWFUL PLACE

What is hell actually like? In Luke 16, we have a graphic description of it. Looking at verses 19 through 31, we have a rare, behind-the-scenes glimpse of what life is like beyond the grave:

133

> "There was a certain rich man, who was clothed in purple and fine linen, and lived in luxury every day: but there was a certain beggar named Lazarus, full of sores, who was laid at his gate, desiring to be fed with the crumbs which fell from the rich man's table: moreover the dogs came and licked his sores.
>
> "And so it was that the beggar died, and was carried by the angels into Abraham's bosom; the rich man also died, and was buried; and being in torment in Hades he lifted up his eyes, and saw Abraham afar off, and Lazarus in his bosom. And he cried and said, 'Father Abraham have mercy on me, and send Lazarus that he may dip the tip of his finger in water, and cool my tongue; for I am tormented in this flame.'
>
> "But Abraham said, 'Son, remember that in your lifetime you received your good things, and likewise Lazarus evil things: but now he is comforted, and you are tormented. Beside all this, between us there is a great gulf fixed: so that those

who want to pass from here to you cannot; nor can those from there pass to us.'

"He said, 'I beg you therefore, father, that you would send him to my father's house: for I have five brothers; that he may testify to them, lest they also come to this place of torment.' Abraham said to him, 'They have Moses and the prophets; let them hear them.' He said, 'No, father Abraham: but if one goes back to them from the dead, they will repent.' He said, 'If they do not hear Moses and the prophets, neither will they be persuaded, though one rises from the dead.'"

This story is not a parable. A parable is an illustration, not an actual event necessarily, but this is not a parable. When Jesus used such illustrations, He would say, "Now learn a parable." This story begins with "A certain man..." This was not just a man in general, but a certain man. Not only that, one of the men in this story is specifically named. His name is Lazarus. Jesus is telling an actual story. This really happened! Here is an incredible, behind-the-scenes glimpse at the Invisible World.

Jesus was addressing people who were obsessed with greed and materialism, people possessed by possessions. He described a certain rich man who "lived in luxury." Obviously, this was a man of means, with considerable resources at his disposal.

When it says he was clothed with "purple" it referred to clothing of royalty, the best material one could buy. "Fine linen" would reaffirm that. The man's attire was the equivalent of "designer clothing" today. This man not only had wealth, he flaunted it. Some people have a lot of money, but they don't have a need to talk about it. They don't brag about it. They don't boast about their bank balances. They don't brag about the material goods they have. They don't remind you what kind of cars they drive. They just have these things.

There are other people who want everybody to know their net worth. They engrave their name on every one of their possessions. They have to let you know what is theirs. They want to tell you about all the things they have and how much they cost. I find that the epitome of tackiness.

I read a description of Howard Hughes written by Bill Hybells. Howard Hughes was one of the richest men who ever lived. All Hughes really wanted in life was "more."

> He wanted more money so he parlayed inherited wealth into a billion dollar pile of assets.

> He wanted more fame so he broke into the Hollywood scene and became a film maker and star.

> He wanted more sensual pleasures so he paid handsome sums to indulge his every sexual urge.

135

> He wanted more thrills so he designed, built, and piloted the fastest aircraft in the world. (You can still go down to Long Beach, California and see the Spruce Goose that he built.)

> He wanted more power so he secretly dealt political favors so skillfully that two U. S. Presidents became his pawns.

All Howard Hughes ever wanted was more. He was absolutely convinced that "more" would bring him true satisfaction. History reveals something altogether different. Toward the end of his life, he was emaciated, colorless, with a sunken chest and fingernails that grew into grotesque, inch-long corkscrews. He had rotting black teeth. He had tumors. He had innumerable needle marks resulting from his drug addiction. He died a billionaire junkie, insane by all reasonable standards. Howard Hughes died, believing the Myth of More.

When Howard Hughes died, he faced death exactly like the poorest man faces it. It didn't matter how much money he had in the bank. It didn't matter how many accomplishments he had achieved in life. Death is the great humbler. It brings us all to one level.

The man in this true story Jesus told also lived in the lap of luxury, and flamboyantly flaunted his wealth. Meanwhile, outside his gate was this impoverished man named Lazarus. Lazarus ate the crumbs from this man's table. In that culture, the affluent person would wipe his hands on pieces of bread and throw the bread away. That was Lazarus' diet. How pathetic: a poor man eating the bread a rich man used to wipe his hands.

We also read that Lazarus was carried and laid at the gate, so perhaps he was crippled, too. The story continues,

> "The beggar died, and was carried by the angels to Abraham's bosom: the rich man also died and was buried."

136

The angels carried Lazarus to heaven, something that didn't happen to the rich man. The rich man's sin was not wealth. His sin was disregard for spiritual values which revealed itself in his prideful flaunting of resources and his neglect of a starving, disabled man at his door.

As is always the case, they both faced death. No doubt the rich man had a lavish funeral that would make the news today. It really didn't matter because his next stop wasn't so glamorous. It was Hades, and he was in torment there.

Hades Changed When Jesus Came

What is Hades? It's neither hell nor the lake of fire. Hades, prior to the crucifixion and resurrection of Jesus Christ, was divided into two compartments: comfort and torment. When a righteous man died under the old covenant, before the coming of the Messiah, he went into Abraham's bosom.

Abraham was the great patriarch of the Jewish people; a man of faith. To go into his bosom meant that you went to the place Abraham went. You went into the presence of God. We're told that those who died in faith, before the arrival of Jesus, were waiting. In faith, they were waiting for the arrival of the Messiah. When Jesus died on the cross, He went to Hades and took the people in that place of comfort into heaven with Him.

As Jesus was hanging on the cross, the thief next to Him said, "Lord, remember me when you come into your kingdom." Jesus said, "Today you will be with me in paradise (Luke 23:42-43)." It would appear that this man got to watch the whole amazing process firsthand. Talk about being in the right place at the right time! First, he's hanging on a cross next to Jesus. Then, he's down there in Hades seeing all those people who had died in faith. Next, he joins them as Jesus escorts them all to heaven.

From that moment forward Hades continued to exist, but only as a place of torment. Even today, if you are a nonbeliever and die, you will go to this place called Hades. The word *torment* is used four times in this account.

You might ask, "Greg, do you really believe that? I mean literally?" I believe it's just as bad, if not worse, as the description in the Bible. One thing I know. It is a horrible place to be. The worst thing about it is that God will not be there. If you go there, you will be separated from Him for all eternity.

137

People Are Conscious There

This story tells us that when you are in Hades, you are conscious. When someone dies, we say that person is dead. In reality, the body is dead, but the spirit lives on. The "real you" is not the shell you live in called the body. This is dramatically evident when a person dies. You look at the body, and though it looks like the person you once knew, the spark of life is gone. That which gave character, personality and uniqueness to that individual is no longer there. You're just looking at a shell. The real person has departed.

People Are In Pain There

In Hades, people are fully conscious. There is even an ability to communicate. It also is a place of great pain. This man is so alarmed by this situation, he wants to get word back to his brothers. Reread verse 28 where he says,

> "'I have five brothers; send Lazarus that he may
> testify to them, lest they also come to this place of
> torment.' Abraham said to him, 'They have Moses
> and the prophets; let them hear them.' And he said,

'No, father Abraham: but if one goes back to them from the dead, they will repent.'"

The rich man didn't say, "I'm having a great time and I'm glad my brothers are coming here to join me. We'll party." In hell there will be no partying. There will be torture, suffering and eternal separation from God.

THERE IS LIFE AFTER DEATH

He said, "What if somebody were to arise from the dead." How many times have we read in a market tabloid about claims of out-of-body experiences? Supposedly, people have died. Then, they came back. They often tell us that they saw a great light or that they felt a great peace. Do you think that if these people are telling the truth, they may have been deceived? If they weren't Christians, no "great light" or "great peace" is waiting. Could it be that Satan, who appears as an angel of light, appeared to them and deceived them? That way, they could come back after their brief sojourn and say that everything is fine, giving false hope and assurance.

I'm amazed at how many people will hang on the words of individuals who supposedly have left the body and come back again. Yet, they reject wholesale the words of the living God who has been there and returned to tell us exactly what we can expect. The reason we reject His words is because we don't like them. They don't agree with the lifestyles we have chosen.

The rich man said, "If someone rose from the dead, they would believe." As as matter of fact, a man did rise from the dead and his name was also Lazarus (a different Lazarus than we read about here). And when Lazarus rose from the dead, what did the religious leaders do? They plotted to kill him! Here was the miracle of miracles, a dead man alive again, and the religious authorities wanted to eliminate him because he was living evidence of the power of God.

Someone even greater than Lazarus also rose from the dead. His name was Jesus. Did that turn the hearts of all the nonbelievers back to God? Not at all. Even a resurrection won't do it. We might think, "If only I could do a miracle for my nonbelieving friends and family to see. If I could walk over to some blind person and open their eyes, they'd believe. All my friends would come to the Lord." Jesus said,

> "A wicked and adulterous generation seeks after a
> sign, but no sign will be given them but that of the
> prophet Jonah that as Jonah was three days and
> three nights in the stomach of the whale so will the
> Son of Man be three days and three nights in the
> heart of the earth (Matthew 12:39-40)."

Jesus was saying, "Here's my sign: Just as Jonah went into the whale and emerged three days later, I am going to die and rise again from the dead. That's your sign."

We wish we could dazzle the world with miracles, but the greatest truth we have to share with those outside of the faith is the simple truth that Jesus went to the cross, died and rose again from the dead. If they will trust Him and follow Him, their sins will be forgiven. Don't underestimate the power of the message of the gospel. Paul says,

139

> "We preach Christ crucified. We don't want to
> know anything else among you except Jesus Christ
> and Him crucified."

That's the message people need. You may say, "Show me and I'll believe." God essentially says, "Believe and I'll show you."

EVENTS OF THE LAST DAYS

The Rapture

Hades, that horrible place of torment, still exists today. Those that are there will receive final judgment after the return of Christ but a few other things have to happen first. The next event on the prophetic calendar will be the Rapture of the Church. The Lord Himself will descend from heaven and take those of us who believe in Him to be with Him.

> Two will be grinding at a mill;
> > one will be taken, the other left.
> Two will be asleep in a bed;
> > one will be taken and the other left.

Two will be working in a field;
  one will be taken, the other left.

The Lord will catch us up to be with Him. We will be changed into incorruptible beings in a moment, in the twinkling of an eye.

The Great Tribulation

Then will come the Antichrist. This world leader, this man of peace, will bring about a one world monetary system, a one world government, and a one world religion. With ten nations confederated under him, he will become the supreme leader of a dominant world power.

Also, there will be a seven year period the Bible calls, "The Great Tribulation." During the first three-and-a-half years, the Antichrist will dazzle the world with his talk of peace. He will even be able to bring a pseudo-peace for this planet. Then, after another three-and-a-half years, the Bible tells us that, "When they say peace and safety, sudden destruction will come upon them as upon a woman in travail." Halfway into the Tribulation the antichrist will show his true colors. God's judgment will fall powerfully upon mankind for the remainder of that period. The Great Tribulation will culminate when the antichrist and his forces meet God's army in one terrible, final war; the Battle of Armegeddon.

The Millenium

After that, Jesus will set up His kingdom. The Invisible and Visible Worlds will merge together. When He returns, He will come with His angels and He will be accompanied by true believers. You and I, who have trusted in Christ, will return with Him. We call this period of time, "The Millennium." Jesus will govern this recreated planet for a thousand years. You and I, as Christians, will rule and reign with Him.

Satan's Final Judgment

Satan will be chained up, and after a thousand years, he will be released for a short time. Then, as Revelation 20:10 says,

The devil that deceived the whole world was cast into the lake of fire and brimstone, where the beast and the false prophet are, and they will be tormented day and night forever and ever.

Then, it will be Satan's day of reckoning. His day of judgment will finally come. He will be dealt with appropriately. That's it for Lucifer.

The Great White Throne Judgment

What about those nonbelievers who have died? They have been in Hades up to this point, in continuing torment. Revelation 20:11-15 says,

I saw a great white throne, and Him that sat on it, from whose face the earth and the heaven fled away; and there was found no place for them. And I saw the dead, small and great, stand before God; and the books [plural] were opened: and another book [singular] was opened, which is the book of life: and the dead were judged according to their works by the things which were written in the books. The sea gave up the dead which were in it; and death and hell delivered up the dead which were in them: and they were judged each one according to his works. And death and Hades were cast into the lake of fire. This is the second death. Anyone not found written in the book of life was cast into the lake of fire.

A word of warning: if you find yourself standing there, you've gone too far. There's no more hope for you. If you think you're going to plead your case in front of the Great White Throne and get off the hook, it's not going to work. Verse 12 tells us the small and the great will be gathered there. God is no respecter of persons. It doesn't matter to Him that some of the people that will stand before Him were world leaders. Maybe they were once presidents or celebrities, emperors or intellectuals, dictators or millionaires. It won't matter.

On this grim occasion, only nonbelievers will be present. Christians aren't mentioned there. I think it would be a dreadful thing to observe such a spectacle. It would certainly spoil heaven for me, especially if I saw loved ones standing there and understood the fate that awaited them. You might ask, "If the nonbeliever is judged already, why is he here?" Jesus said,

> "He that believes in Me is not condemned, but he who does not believe in Me is condemned already because he has not believed in the name of the only begotten Son of the God."

142

If they're condemned already, why do they stand before the judgment seat of God? What's the point? Perhaps it is to clearly demonstrate to the nonbeliever the reason for his judgment. You can be sure that somebody will say, "Unfair! This isn't right!" But, the books are open. What is contained in these books? We don't know. We can only imagine.

Other passages of Scripture seem to indicate that perhaps one of these books will be a record of everything we've ever said or done. You say, "Hey, I'm a good person. I lived a good life. I was kind and considerate to my fellow man. I really never did anything bad enough to deserve this." Consider that everything you have ever said and done has been recorded. Ecclesiastes 12:14 says, "God will judge us for everything we do including every hidden thing good or bad."

Every thought, every word, every action will be made public for everyone to see. Somewhere in your life, you've done something that could be classified as sin. We would be more accurate if we admitted that we commit many sins every day. It's all recorded.

Another book may be the book of the law. Some people say, "I lived by the Ten Commandments. That's all I needed to do." All right, let's take a look at the whole law and see how you fare. If the book of the law is brought out, it will show that we're all guilty. Romans 3:19 says, "The purpose of the law is to shut every mouth that all the world may become guilty before God."

The purpose of the Law is to show us we need a Savior. If you try to live by the rules and regulations of the law of Moses, you will find out that you fall short. We all fail. No one can live up to it.

By its very design, the law was designed to drive us to Christ and to make us realize we can't possibly keep the rules!

There may be another book that has a record of every time you've heard the gospel and rejected it. Knowledge brings responsibility. I'm sure in heaven they'll have something far greater than video technology. If they do, I'll guarantee that you won't be looking at *Heaven's Funniest Home Videos!* It might be more like a version of the well–known, old T.V. program, *This is Your Life*. You may be taken back to when you first heard the gospel. Here you are as a four year old in Sunday school, hearing about Jesus for the first time. That's you in the back of the room. While the teacher is speaking about Jesus, you're the one cutting off the little girl's pony tail!

143

The next scene shows you getting a little older. Your Mom is telling you about Jesus. She's telling you that you need to pray, but you're not interested. You don't want to hear it.

Now, we see you at church. It's a little bit later in life, and you really don't want to be there. You're sitting in the back, laughing and goofing off with your friends.

Still later, you are changing the channels on the television set. There is a preacher on the screen, pointing his long finger at you and telling you that you need Christ. You just keep turning the channel because you'd rather watch something else.

Here you are now, reading this book, being presented with the gospel once again. Are you thinking to yourself, "I really don't want to finish this book. It bothers me." You're disinterested... unconcerned. You may be saying, "There will be other opportunities. I'll get around to God later. I want to have some fun first."

Death hits without warning. There is no knock on your door. It just happens. It's over with. Those nail-scarred hands will open the Book of Life and search for your name. Is it there? Will Jesus say sadly, "Depart from me, I never knew you. I'm sending you into eternal fire, which is prepared for the devil and his angels." Some will protest, "Lord, Lord, didn't I prophesy in your name? In your name, didn't I do many wonderful works?" He says, "I never knew you. I never knew you. I never knew you." Those chilling words will ring in the condemned person's ears for all eternity.

If you don't know Him now, He won't know you then.

CHAPTER
10

The Hope Of Heaven

Hundreds of years ago, Job asked, "If a man dies, does he go on living?" That same question is still being asked today. We've already considered the subject of the afterlife as it relates to hell, but what about heaven?

We already pointed out that Jesus had more to say about hell than all other preachers of the Bible combined. The Bible describes hell as a place of outer darkness. A place of torment, where the fire is not quenched. A place, most notably, where God is absent. Hell is separation from God for all eternity. It was not prepared for people, but for the devil and his angels. Above all, it's the last place God wants any man or woman to go.

However, if you have accepted Christ and have the assurance of salvation, then hell isn't for you. Talking about death should not be a frightening subject. Like Paul, you can say, "Death, where is your sting? Grave, where is your victory?" We believers know that death is merely a mode of transportation that will get us to the place we long for most: heaven. When believers die, their passage to heaven is direct, with no stopovers.

Some people teach that, at death, we enter into a "soul sleep." Others believe we go into purgatory. The Bible says that believers are ushered directly into the presence of God.

We saw that illustrated in Jesus' story about Lazarus and the rich man after their deaths. Lazarus was immediately carried by the angels into Abraham's bosom.

We also know that the thief on the cross hanging next to Jesus said, "Lord, remember me when you come into your kingdom." And Jesus replied, "Today you will be with me in paradise."

Paul said in Philippians 1:23, "My desire is to depart and be with Christ." He knew as soon as he left His earthly body he would be in the presence of the Lord. He also said,

> "We are always confident and know that as long as we are home in this body, we are away from the Lord. We live by faith and not by sight. We are confident, I say, and would prefer to be away from the body and at home with the Lord."

HEAVEN IS A WONDERFUL PLACE

When we leave this human frame in which our spirit lives, we will go into God's presence.

There's a glimpse of heaven found in Revelation 21:1-8.

> I saw a new heaven and a new earth: for the first heaven and the first earth were passed away; and there was no more sea. And I, John, saw the holy city, new Jerusalem coming down from God out of heaven, prepared as a bride adorned for her husband. And I heard a loud voice out of heaven saying, "Behold, the tabernacle of God is with men, and He will dwell with them, and they shall be His people, and God Himself will be with them, and be their God. And God shall wipe away all tears from their eyes; and there shall be no more death, neither sorrow, nor crying, neither shall there be any more pain: for the former things are passed away." And He that sat upon the throne said, "Behold, I make all things new." And he said unto me, "Write: for these words are true and faithful." And He said unto me, "It is done. I am Alpha and Omega, the beginning and the end. I will give of the fountain of the water of life freely to him that thirsts. He that overcomes shall inherit all things; and I will be his God, and he shall be my son. But the cowardly, and unbelieving, and the abominable, and murders, and sexually immoral, and sorcerers, and idolaters, and all liars, shall have their part in the lake which burns with fire and brimstone: which is the second death."

147

HEAVEN IS A PLACE PREPARED FOR US

When you travel to a place you've never been to before, you want to know a little bit about it. You want to do some study, some preparation. What are the best hotels? What about food? Where are the good restaurants? What should I wear? What's the climate like? What am I going to do when I get there?

Let's think about our heavenly destination for a moment. What about our accommodations? Where are we going to stay? Don't worry about that. Remember Jesus said,

> "In my Father's house are many mansions. If it were not so I would have told you. If I go, I will come again, for I have prepared a place for you."

That's good enough for me. When He says He's prepared a place for me, I know it's going to be the best.

148

What about restaurants? The Bible says we'll be honored guests at the marriage feast of the Lamb.

What about clothes? The Bible tells us that we'll be given a wedding garment. It says that the church will be arrayed in fine linen, clean and bright. Fine linen represents the righteousness of the saints.

What are the sights we are going to view when we get there? How about the sea of glass? How about the river of the water of life clear as crystal flowing from the throne of God and the Lamb? What will we do in heaven? How about lunch with the Apostle Paul or the Prophet Elijah? How about tea with Esther, Deborah and Mary? Martha can serve!

Needless to say, heaven is far more than all these things. Heaven is seeing Jesus Himself! He's what it's all about. He's the highlight of heaven. He's the One I want to meet. Once we arrive, the first thing we'll do is go to the throne of God. D. L. Moody said, "It's not the jeweled walls or the pearly gates that are going to make heaven attractive. It's being with God." I agree with that. The Bible says right now we "see through a glass darkly." It's hard to make it all out. Later, we will see Him face–to–face.

THE THRONE OF THE LAMB

Revelation 7:9-12 gives us an insight into our activities in heaven. It says,

> There was a great multitude, which no man could number, of all nations, and peoples, standing before throne of the Lamb, clothed with white robes, palms

in their hands; crying with a loud voice, saying, "Salvation to our God which sits upon the throne, and unto the Lamb. Blessing and glory, and wisdom, and thanksgiving, and honor and power, and might, be unto our God for ever and ever."

When we see Jesus, we will fall at His feet and worship Him. We will see Him as He is. Revelation says, "For Thy pleasure Thou hast created all things. Thou art worthy, oh Lord." Once we see His face we will surely want to spend a lot of time glorifying and praising Him.

Mansions in Heaven

When you read in the Bible about mansions in heaven, you shouldn't think it's describing an up-scale, middleclass neighborhood with neatly mowed lawns thinking that, if you didn't walk close to the Lord on earth, you'll live in the tract home section. You may even be worrying that, if you barely get by, you'll have a tent somewhere out in a field. When we read about "many mansions," we need to realize that a better translation would be, "In my Father's house are many dwelling places." Jesus was describing the new bodies God has prepared for us when we get there. II Corinthians 5:1 says,

> Now we know if the earthly tent we live in is destroyed we have a building from God, an eternal house in heaven not made with human hands. Meanwhile we groan, longing to be clothed with our heavenly bodies.

As we get older, we do more and more groaning. We groan when we get out of bed in the morning. We drop something, bend over to pick it up and we groan. We go out to play basketball with the kids and pay for it for three weeks as our aging bodies recover. The human body is getting older every day.

Glory in Heaven

It's hard for us to get an accurate picture of what heaven is all about. Paul did his best to describe a short visit he made there. We don't know how this visit came about or when it happened. It may have occurred while Paul was attacked for preaching in the city, when he was stoned and left for dead. It is possible that on that occasion Paul had the incredible glimpse of heaven that he writes about in II Corinthians 12:4. Paul tells us,

> I heard unspeakable words which it is impossible
> for a man to utter. How can I declare it unto you? It
> was paradise.

Have you ever gone to a very beautiful place and taken photographs? When you come back and show them to all your friends, it just isn't the same. The colors aren't as rich as the picture etched in your memory. Your friends aren't able to see it the way you did. Personally, no matter how beautiful the scene, I will always manage to ruin the picture when I take photos. I have a camera that is idiot-proof and I still ruin the picture. You may remember the spectacular sunset in your mind's eye. When you look at the little photographs, it just looks like an ordinary sky.

Imagine Paul having been in heaven, then coming back to earth and trying to describe it to people. It's beyond your wildest dreams. The Bible describes heaven with words like "emerald" and "glass," "crystal." "gold" and "pearls." Think of the Grand Canyon, Hawaii, and the Rocky Mountains. All of these extraordinary places are insignificant compared to heaven.

God can tell us about heaven in Scripture and we try to picture it, but it's beyond us. It's going to be incredible. In heaven there will be no night. Revelation 22:5 says, "There will be no night there. They need no lamp nor light of the sun for the Lord God gives them light."

There will be no fear. We won't need locks on the door, bars on the windows or alarm systems. Everything that causes fear will be eliminated. We'll walk the streets of gold with no concern for danger. The Bible tells us there will be no more suffering or death. Note again Revelation 21 where it says,

> "The dwelling place of God is with man. He will
> wipe every tear from their eyes. There will be no

death or mourning or crying or pain for He makes everything new."

There will be no fear of losing what you have. People won't lose their jobs or their loved ones. Kids won't rebel. Cars won't break down. No one will get sick. No one will die. It will be perfection!

Answers in Heaven

In heaven all of our questions will be answered. Sometimes people say, "When I get to heaven, I'm going to ask God a few questions." I can see it now. As soon as you arrive in glory, you're going to demand, "Where's God?" You're going to storm right up to the throne of the Creator of the Universe, past the adoring, prostrate throngs, and blurt out, "Cut the worship. Hi Lord, I'm here and I've got a few questions for You. I'd like to know why You allowed certain things to happen in my earthly life..."

No, when you get to heaven you'll take one look at Jesus sitting on His throne all–knowing, all–powerful, pure love, and your questions will melt away. You'll say, "Oh, never mind." It will all make sense. All of your questions will be answered.

"Now we see through a glass darkly but then we will see face–to–face. Now I know in part but then I will know even as I am known."

I can't understand everything about God nor can you. God allows things in our lives that don't make sense. Don't allow those circumstances to fill your mind with doubt or to cause you to say that God doesn't know what He's doing. Recognize that there are certain concerns that your finite mind cannot grasp, especially when it comes to dealing with the Infinite God. We have to take some things by faith and trust that God knows what He is doing.

Judgment in Heaven

I Corinthians 3:10-16 deals with a very important area that every Christian will face when he gets to heaven. You might call this the final exam, and I want you to pass with flying colors.

"According to the grace of God which is given to me, as a wise master builder, I have laid the foundation, and another builds on it. But let each one take heed how he builds on it. For no other foundation can be laid than that which is Jesus Christ.

"Now if any one builds upon this foundation with gold, silver, precious stones, wood, hay, or stubble; every man's work will become clear: for the day will declare it, because it shall be revealed by fire; and the fire shall test each one's work of what sort it is. If any man's work which he has built endures, he will receive a reward. If any man's work is burned, he shall suffer loss: but he himself will be saved; yet so as by fire.

"Know ye not that ye are the temple of God, and that the Spirit of God dwells within you?" (I Corinthians 3:10-16).

This is called the Judgment Seat of Christ. In the last chapter, we dealt with what the Bible calls the Great White Throne Judgment. That is the final judgment for nonbelievers—those who have rejected Christ. But, believers will not be at the Great White Throne Judgment.

Rewards

The Judgment Seat of Christ has nothing to do with whether or not we will get into heaven. We've already made it there! This judgment deals with rewards. The Judgment Seat of Christ in the original language is called the "bema" seat. That may not mean much to us, but in the ancient Olympic games, the "bema" seat was where the judge sat. After a contestant had won the race, he would come before the judge and receive a crown. The same words are used by Paul. We will receive rewards in heaven. Paul said,

"I have fought the good fight. I finished the course. I kept the faith. Henceforth there is laid up for me a crown of righteousness and not to me only but to all who love His appearing."

If you are looking forward to the return of Christ and living in anticipation of it, God will give you a crown of righteousness. There is also the promise in Scripture of a crown of life, given to those who endure hardships. Other crowns are mentioned in Scripture as well.

Every one of us is different. God has invested certain abilities, gifts and talents in each of our lives. The "bema" seat judgment will determine how well we invested the gifts and talents He gave us. What did you do with your life? What did you do with your time?

153

We may be surprised to see that certain philanthropists on earth who are known for great acts of benevolence will receive nothing at all. They will get no rewards, no crowns, because they enjoyed all their accolades on earth. Jesus warns of that trap: giving so people will see what you gave. Sometimes when a person presents a gift, he'll leave the price tag on it. He's making an announcement: "Hey, did everyone see what I just gave him? I paid a lot of money for it. I'm such a generous guy!"

Some organizations offer to put your name on a pillar or a pane of glass or some other "living memorial" if you make a large enough donation. Then, everybody can walk by and say, "My, my! Just look how much that person gave!" You may never hear about the widow who gave two pennies, but in heaven, she'll probably have a front row seat. Meanwhile, the great philanthropist may not be mentioned at all. Jesus said, "When you give, don't let your right hand know what your left hand is doing."

A loose paraphrase might be, "Keep your mouth shut and just do it." Your Father who sees you in secret will one day reward you openly. That promise is for some of you who have faithfully served the Lord without fanfare. No one knows your name, but you quietly do the Lord's work, anyway. When you get to heaven you're going to be rewarded. God sees everything you do. He sees every sacrifice you've made. He sees everything you've done quietly for the glory of God. He knows you haven't been seeking your own glory or the applause of man.

There will be those at the "bema" seat who gave only when it was convenient; who served only when they were in the mood; who cooperated only if their own interests were served. These individuals are going to receive very little. The fire of God's judgment will burn away their false motives. Those good deeds prompted by self-interest (wood, hay or stubble) are going to be scorched very quickly.

Motives

The "bema" seat will be a judgment of motives. The only valid reason to serve God is love. Paul said, "No matter what I do; if I allow my body to be burned, if I have faith to move mountains, if I give up everything I own, if it is not motivated by love it means nothing." What a test! I wonder how many of us will stand with shame before God. Paul says, "I want to have an abundant entrance into the kingdom of God."

The way some Christians live out their years on earth, squandering their life, time and resources, you would think when they die and go to heaven, they will just want to quietly slip in the back door. You're going to stand before God and He's going to say, "What did you do with your life? What did you live for? Did you use your abilities merely to be successful, popular, powerful or to amass money?" In that final day, some will have a saved soul but a lost life. I want to get to heaven and stand before the One who gave everything for me and say, "Lord, here's what I did. I know this doesn't merit what You did for me. I know I haven't earned my way in. That's only through what Jesus did. But Lord, I did this for Your glory and I loved every moment of it. I offer it to You."

Will there be people in heaven because you invited them... because you prayed for them... because you shared with them? Think about it. Consider it. One day very soon, we're going to stand before God. Don't let the precious opportunities that God gives you slip by.

Commitment

You say, "Greg, I don't have a lot to give to the Lord." Join the club! God didn't get some great catch when I gave my life to Him as a seventeen year old boy. I had very little to offer. Five loaves and two fishes would sum it up, if that much. I was just a boy, but I knew that I had been forgiven and I wanted to serve Him. So, I offered what little I had. I said, "Lord, here I am." Anything God has accomplished through my life is a direct result of His power and glory. If you will offer what you have, no matter how much or how little, you'll be amazed as you watch what God will do with it.

So, we have the choice: the "bema" seat or the Great White Throne. There are no second chances. The Bible says, "It is appointed unto man once to die and after this the judgment."

155

Hopefully we'll all be safe in heaven, joyfully receiving our rewards.

ON THE OUTSIDE LOOKING IN

Cowardice

Who will be outside? In Revelation 6, we read that the fearful will be out there. Another way to translate the word "fearful" is "cowardly." This probably refers to those who never stood up and became a Christian for fear of others. Isn't it ridiculous to think that some people won't come to Christ because they're afraid of what others might think?

Pilate

Pontius Pilate had Jesus Himself standing before him, and he didn't believe Jesus was guilty. Pilate wasn't at all happy with the situation because he had to make a decision about what to do with Jesus. In his heart, Pilate knew He was innocent. Furthermore, his wife had warned him to have nothing to do with this righteous man. Pilate thought, "What am I going to do?" The crowds were screaming, "Crucify Him!" So, Pilate let the others make his decision for him. He did not do what was right; he did what was popular. He sentenced Jesus to death. Then, he dipped his hands in a basin of water and said, "I wash my hands of this matter." Sorry, Pilate, you can't wash the blood of Jesus Christ off your hands.

Pilate made the biggest mistake a person can make when it comes to personal spiritual decisions. He let the people vote and went with the popular consensus. Much of the time the crowd is wrong.

Broad is the way that leads to destruction and many there are that go that way.

The Bible says,"All we like sheep have gone astray and turned everyone to his own way."

Don't follow the crowd. Decide for yourself.

Simon Peter

After the Lord was arrested and taken to be tried, Peter was warming himself at a nearby fire. A young servant girl came up to him and said, "You're one of those disciples of Jesus aren't you?" Peter denied it. Ultimately, he cursed and said, "I never knew the man!" He was afraid of what other people would think of him. How pathetic his cowardice was. Don't worry about what others think about you. Be concerned with what God thinks about you.

When you stand up on that final day, you're not going to be with your friends. You're going to be all alone. How feeble and absurd it will seem to think that you rejected Jesus because you wanted your friends to think you were cool or because you didn't want to be laughed at.

Outside heaven will be the cowardly. If you're going to follow Jesus Christ, you're going to have to stand up and be counted.

Immorality

We are told that the sexually immoral are outside heaven, too. "Sexually immoral" comes from the Greek word "porniea," the root of our English word pornographic. This word is broad in its implication. It refers to those who are involved in sex outside of marriage.

In God's estimation, the only proper sexual context is within the marriage relationship. If you have sexual intercourse before marriage or outside of marriage, or if you take part in homosexual relations or incest, you are violating God's order. God says those that practice such things will not inherit the kingdom of God. That's very important. If you're practicing these right now, God says you're not going to enter heaven. You'd better repent.

You say, "I'm doing it! Am I out for good?" It doesn't have to be permanent, you can repent. If you ask God to forgive you and break off your immoral relationships, God will forget your sin. There's hope for you. Jesus died on the cross for your sin, but if you continue sinning saying, "I went forward at an invitation to follow Jesus in church a year ago. I'm okay," you're deceiving yourself. The Bible says if you continue in these things you'll not inherit the kingdom of God.

Sorcery

Outside heaven are sorcerers. These guys aren't necessarily **157** wearing pointed hats with stars on them and carrying crystal balls. Sorcery, in the Bible, is an interesting word. It comes from a Greek root, from which we get our English word "pharmacy." Sorcery means "an enchantment with drugs." This would include those who are involved in drug abuse. Those who are involved with drugs are left outside heaven.

Idolatry

Idolaters are outside too. This isn't just people who bow themselves before wooden images. These are people that have allowed anything or anyone to take the place of supreme devotion to God in their lives.

An idol can be many things.

 It can be a relationship.

 It can be a career.

 It can be a possession, a car, a house, anything.

 It can be yourself.

If you think the universe revolves around you and what you want and think, remember that idolaters will be outside heaven.

Lies

Outside heaven will be liars. That category speaks for itself. Jesus said you know a tree by its fruit. Check out the fruit. Some people get really angry when you say, "I don't know if you're really a Christian." "Hey, don't judge me," they protest. "Remember, the Bible says, 'Judge not lest you be judged.'"

You might respond, "O.K., think of it as fruit inspection. I don't see very good fruit coming out of your life."

CHOOSE YOUR LEADER

Are you involved in the things we've listed? Do you think you're pulling the wool over God's eyes? He sees everything. He knows everything. You can't fool Him. You can fool all of the people some of the time and some of the people all of the time, but you can't fool God any of the time. There's an engraving on the wall of a cathedral in Germany that says,

158

"Thus speaketh Christ our Lord to us:

You call Me Master and obey Me not.
　　You call Me Light and see Me not.
You call Me the Way and walk Me not.
　　You call Me Life and live Me not.
You call Me wise and follow Me not.
　　You call Me fair and love Me not.
You call Me rich and ask Me not.
　　You call Me eternal and seek Me not.
If I condemn you, blame Me not."

There will be those in that day who will say, "Lord, Lord! Haven't we done miracles in your name? Haven't we cast out demons in your name?" He'll say, "Depart from me. I never knew you. Why do you call me Lord, Lord and not do the things that I say?"

Liars and hypocrites are only fooling themselves. They might as well just give it up; either get with it or get out. People should either follow the Lord one hundred percent or go for the world one hundred percent. If you're going to go for the world, do it all... live it all... drain it of its last drop, then pay the price and go to hell. At least, you'll have made the most of your life on this earth. You'll have had your fun. You won't have played this stupid religious game deceiving yourself. You'll have had all the thrills you could, well aware that you will pay for it for all eternity.

On the other hand, if you're going to be a Christian, be a Christian! Give your all; one hundred percent, totally committed!

Whatever you do, however, give up this idea of thinking you can live in both worlds. Jesus said, "I want you to be hot or cold. If you're lukewarm, I'll spit you out."

If you don't want to go to heaven, you don't have to, but heaven is the greatest opportunity God could offer you. The Bible says, "How can we escape if we neglect so great a salvation?"

Where do you stand with God right now? As we have looked at the Invisible World and what happens after death, perhaps you've not really been sure where you will spend eternity. Jesus wants you to spend it in heaven with Him; "In His presence will be fullness of joy and at His right hand pleasures for evermore."

Satan doesn't want you to find that hope. He's tried to keep you away from Christ. He's been deceiving you. It's time to come to One who loves you more than anyone else does. The One who knows you better than you know yourself. The One who loved us so much that He went to the cross of Calvary and took the penalty that should have been ours and bore it in our place. His name is Jesus, and He says to you, "Behold, I stand at the door and knock. If you hear my voice and open the door I will come in (Matthew 7:8)."

You can open the door of your life and receive Jesus Christ as your personal Lord and Savior right now. Pray this prayer:

"Lord Jesus, forgive me of my sin. I know I am a sinner. I thank You that You died for my sin and rose from the dead. I want You to be my personal Lord and Savior. Write my name in Your Book of Life and fill me with your Spirit. Thank You for forgiving me. Thank You that I am now a child of God and that I am now going to heaven. In Jesus' name I pray. Amen."

If you've prayed that prayer, Christ has come into your life. Write and let me know. I'll send you some helpful materials to encourage you in your spiritual growth.

GREG LAURIE
6115 Arlington
Riverside, CA 92504